"My friend Norm Miller is a unique person—certainly one of the most down-to-earth, honest, and spontaneous business executives I've ever met. In *Beyond the Norm* you see not only what makes this fun guy tick, but also the core principles and values of a man who knows how to make the most out of business and life."

Tom Landry,
former head coach of
the Dallas Cowboys

"*Beyond the Norm* is an important book for the person in today's fast-paced, competitive business world. Through his personal experience, Norm Miller illustrates to us that it is possible to merge our aggressive, ambitious, and creative drive with our spiritual and humanitarian side to grow a successful business."

Roger Staubach,
chairman and CEO,
the Staubach Company

"Norm shares some valuable life lessons that provide a great picture of a man God has used in a mighty way. He has made a difference in the lives of thousands of people. His most challenging message is through his personal example of boldness to stand for God in his business."

Steven S. Reinemund,
president and CEO,
Frito-Lay, Inc.

BEYOND THE NORM

NORM MILLER

WITH H. K. HOSIER

THOMAS NELSON PUBLISHERS
Nashville • Atlanta • London • Vancouver

Published in Nashville, Tennessee, by Thomas Nelson, Inc., and distributed in Canada by Word Communications, Ltd., Richmond, British Columbia, and in the United Kingdom by Word (UK), Ltd., Milton Keynes, England.

Library of Congress Cataloging-in-Publication Data

Miller, Norm.
   Beyond the norm / Norm Miller with H.K. Hosier.
      p.   cm.
   Includes bibliographical references (p.).
   ISBN 0-7852-7674-2 (cloth)
   1. Miller, Norm. 2. Businessmen—United States—Biography. 3. Chief executive officers—United States—Biography. 4. Interstate Battery System of America—History. 5. Success in business. 6. Christian life. I. Hosier, Helen Kooiman. II. Title.
HC102.5.M47A3   1996
338.7′629254092—dc20
   [B]   96-11899
                                                                          CIP

Printed in the United States of America

1 2 3 4 5 6 7 - 02 01 00 99 98 97 96

DEDICATION

To all my family—

Lawrence, Ruth, Anne, Tracey, Michael, Zach, Kyle, Scott, Donna, Braden, Grant, Jimmy, Corky (Jean), Ruth Ann, Bill, Brian, Scott, Chris, Larry, Kathy, Jacob, Aaron, Anna, Glenn, Andrea, Matt, Kimmie, Tommy, Scottie, Monika, Melissa, J. D., Austin, Janet, Deanna, Arnold, Jessica, Joshua, Jennifer, Donnie, Sherrie, Desiree, Cody, Courtney, Daylyn, Eleanor, Joan, Steve, Lori, Matt, Paul, Joe, Phyllis, and Freddy

—they've all had a part in this!

ACKNOWLEDGMENTS

As in the case of most books, one person is acknowledged as the author, but many people, working selflessly, actually make it happen. Such is the case with this book.

I want to express my sincere thanks and deep appreciation to Norma Peyton, my secretary; to Jim Cote and Ted Voltmer; and especially to Helen Hosier, Leslie Peterson, and Bruce Nygren; but most of all to my wife, Anne, who has patiently and pleasantly helped me keep at it throughout these many months of writing.

Contents

FOREWORD

Chairman of the board. An impressive title, but to the folks at Interstate Battery, he's simply Ol' Norm. If you knew him, you would know why.

I first met Norm Miller back in 1991 when I flew to Dallas to meet with him about putting together a NASCAR Winston Cup race team. We've been racing together ever since. My football career got me in the door, but our friendship has kept us together.

In the business world, Norm and I are partners. I own the #18 Interstate Batteries car, and Norm's company is the sponsor. If that were all there was to our relationship, it would be no different from thousands of other business relationships in corporate America. The fruits of our partnership are several victories and a top-ten car in the NASCAR circuit. The fruits of our friendship, however, run much deeper. We've vacationed together with our wives and families, and once we actually drove and raced stock cars together with our sons at the Texas World Speedway.

Over time, I've learned that Norm Miller, while having built a very successful company, is not concerned about fitting into the social mold of a top executive. He's more at home in a pair of khakis and a sports shirt than he is in a suit. His unique experiences in business and in life will definitely give you plenty of food for thought. He's a fun, fascinating man, and a person of great faith.

Norm will tell you that his batteries are "built to last." I'll tell you the same thing about our friendship. Read his book, and get to know him. His story is powerful.

Joe Gibbs
Charlotte, North Carolina

PREFACE

At a dinner party more than twenty years ago, as my wife and I were getting acquainted with those we didn't know, someone asked me what I did for a living.

"I sell batteries—Interstate batteries," I responded.

"Car batteries?" another fella questioned. "Aren't they the green ones? I think I have one!"

I told him yes and added that Interstate didn't advertise much, but Dallas was our home territory and we sold over 20 percent of all replacement batteries in the area.

Another guy said, "Hey, let's go look under the hoods of our cars and see if we have any."

So out we trooped. Six car hoods went up, and out of the six, three had Interstate batteries. All right! That sure made my evening!

Even now when we're the number-one-selling replacement battery in North America, I'd be the first to acknowledge that Interstate Battery System of America isn't a household name. Our company doesn't sell to big discount retailers, and we don't manufacture our own batteries. Many of our customers, like the men at that dinner party, aren't aware they have an Interstate battery in their car or truck. But it's true—we are number one in the industry, and we're proud of that. (Hey, you might want to go look under the hood of your own car right now!)

I'm certainly very grateful for what has happened to Interstate Batteries in recent years. In 1995 we reached an all-time high with unit battery sales totaling more than ten million. That's quite a ways from our early days when, in 1965, we were selling about a quarter of a million batteries a year. Today our sales surpass those of Sears Diehard, Delco, and many other nationally recognized names.

Some say we got to this point by being independent and aggressive and by understanding the marketplace. True, we have all worked hard at what we do, including the 343 distributors and more than

200,000 dealers in the United States, Canada, and several other countries. But I know it's more than aggressiveness and business savvy that got us to where we are today, and in this book I'll tell you why.

And there's a lot more than the battery business that I want to share with you. I want to share my own story and some of the important things I've learned along the way. I'll tell about my growing-up years, college, how I met my wife, the joys and challenges of raising a family, how I became a part of Interstate Batteries, and the company's history.

I always feel a little funny talking about myself and Interstate because it's like I'm trying to blow my own horn. That's not my intention. I just hope that some of this story will be helpful and motivating.

$$\sim\!\!\sim\!\!\sim$$

I have a friend who once told me that as a child he used to like to watch kites fly, soaring high on the winds. He'd think to himself, *Some day I want to soar like that kite.* Then he'd think, *If I cut the string, the kite will just soar and fly off into the heavens.*

But that's not reality. If you cut the string, what happens? We've all seen kites that have gotten away from someone on the ground. They wind up crashed in a tree or tangled in some wires. For sure, they don't get anywhere intact on their own.

That's the way it is with life. We need moorings—someone or something to keep us in control. I have to be up front with you and say that after living a very full and interesting life, I want my moorings in faith, and I only want to soar with God. That's where my heart is. But, of course, some days I do better at soaring than others.

My wife, Anne, and I have four grandsons and the other two are only sixteen months apart. We've spent a lot of time with Zach and Kyle. They can go after each other pretty good, just like most boys. When they were smaller tykes, they got into a big fight and Kyle, the younger one, threw a toy car at Zach, hitting him in his stocking foot. The car had some sharp edges, and Zach squalled like a stuck pig. After Anne settled him down, he pulled his sock off, revealing a small puncture wound with a little blood on it. That's when Zach really became upset. Between the sobs he cried, "Grandma, Grandma, put your finger on it. All my air is gonna go out!"

I don't know about y'all (remember, I'm a Texan!), but sometimes I feel like all my air is let out. There are days when I don't soar like I know I could and should. There have been times when it has been very difficult to muster up the courage and strength to go on.

Like most people, I've encountered a lot of problems and challenges in my life, many of them my own doing. I've experienced relationship problems with my children; I've had marriage troubles. There have been problems with alcohol, anger, and rage. With the help of counseling, prayer, and good friends, God has brought me and my family through. Today we're doing great; the relationships are on track to what they should be, and I've learned to take life one day at a time as I try to be faithful to what I know is the Truth and the Way.

During one particularly tough time, a person sent me a little card with black writing on it. The message read:

Go on, don't quit.
Your work is not in vain.
I'll always be with you
to strengthen and sustain.

That really helped me—just a simple, small thing. It was as if God was whispering to me, "Go on, keep on, don't quit. Remember, I love you. Victory is ahead and I will see you through."

How little did I realize then how true those words would be—for the whole of my life.

PART ONE
Trying to Throw the Hook

DAYTONA

Daytona Speed Week. There is little else that can match the energy, sights, sounds, and sheer thrills of the days leading up to the big race—the Daytona 500. It is the Super Bowl of the NASCAR circuit, one of the brightest, most desired "jewels" of automobile racing.

There probably isn't a NASCAR driver who wouldn't agree that winning the Daytona 500 is his greatest dream, but many among the best have never won. Included in that number is Dale Earnhardt, a seven-time Winston Cup champion who, despite sixteen tries, has yet to see the checkered flag at Daytona.

Before you run into the ocean for a swim, you
should first put in your toes, and then your feet,
and then your ankles—slowly.

So in 1993, what was I doing right in the middle of all the excitement of Daytona, and I do mean the middle? I stood in the pit area watching a flourescent-green blur with a big "18" on the side flashing past at over two hundred miles an hour—too fast to read the Interstate Batteries logo written in bold letters on the hood and fenders. The green and black Mike Laughlin Chevy

Lumina, driven by Dale Jarrett, was part of our fledgling two-year-old racing team.

The crew and the crowd of 150,000 erupted in a roar as the race entered the final laps. Just a year earlier in 1992, our first year in NASCAR, we'd gone the whole season without winning a single race. But we knew teamwork and a good car were the keys to success. Now our driver was fighting his way up to second place with only seven laps to go—at the Daytona 500, of all races!

The cheering and shouting grew unbelievably loud. But even as I watched and yelled myself hoarse, I remembered all the long, hard hours of teamwork—a word with a lot behind it—that had gone into getting this far, this fast.

〰〰

Charles Suscavage, the director of public relations at Interstate Batteries, has a philosophy that I can buy into. He says that before you run into the ocean for a swim, you should first put in your toes, and then your feet, and then your ankles—*slowly*. Then you keep working your way out to see if that's where you really want to go.

That's how Interstate became involved in NASCAR Winston Cup racing. It seemed like a good choice for a company in the battery business. Our public relations and advertising folks loved the idea of being racing sponsors, and we could get in at a very good price. "Good PR, good advertising, Norm," the fellows said, so I gave them a thumbs-up and a "Let's go for it!"

We began in 1989 by dipping our toes into the water with a good driver and team owner, Stanley Smith, in the Challenge series. From there we ventured further out into some Busch Grand National and Winston Cup races.

These first steps resulted in a bunch of publicity and name recognition while also whetting our appetite for racing promotion. Our distributors and dealers loved it and were cheering us on.

In 1991, when we became the number one replacement brand

battery in America, I started hearing, "Hey Norm, *now* can we get a number one race car too?"

I appreciated their push to get more competitive, run up front, and win some races. But I figured any big changes were still pretty far down the road.

IT ALL STARTED IN APRIL

The shallow water that we had dipped our toes into, however, soon became a wave that swept us along into the deep water of the real racing world, ready or not. It started in April 1991 with a phone call out of the blue from Joe Gibbs of the Washington Redskins, one of the winningest coaches in the National Football League. I was and am a fan of Joe's, knowing him mostly by his accomplishments as an extremely successful coach with three Super Bowl championships, four NFL championships, five division titles, seven play-off teams, and two Associated Press Coach of the Year awards! Needless to say, a call from Joe was a big surprise; I could not figure out why he would be calling me.

Joe told me that he was putting together a NASCAR Winston Cup racing team, and while he knew we were already part-time sponsors of one car, Max Helton (chaplain to the NASCAR family through Motor Racing Outreach) had told him that we were "good people." Would we be interested in moving up to a full-time competitive team? Joe wanted to put together a team of solid people committed to winning, and he would like the opportunity to present his plan and sponsorship package to us.

I have to be honest and say that decision making can sometimes be awfully difficult, and this decision was no exception. Even though I'm a man who has a strong faith in God, most of the time I don't have special illumination—so I do try to follow certain guidelines. I study the Bible; I know the difference between right and wrong; and I know how to get things done.

So when I'm presented with an opportunity like the one Joe Gibbs was offering, after specific prayer, I ask myself, "Should you do it?"

and "Can you do it?" If the answer to both questions is yes, I'm ready to say, "Then do it!"

Joe Gibbs's call left me with a good, positive impression. I gave him an immediate okay to a meeting. Joe said it would take him three to four weeks to get the package together before he could come to Dallas and present it to us. Then he added, "I won't make a deal until you get a look at it, Norm." That surprised me and made me feel really good; it also confirmed my hunch that this might be a good deal in the making.

Within ten days Joe was on the phone again. Prospective sponsors were already getting anxious, and he wanted to come down as soon as possible.

Every race is exciting, but even experienced sportswriters and longtime observers rated the 1993 race as the best Daytona 500 in history.

Joe came, and we hit it off immediately. He was fun. He laughs and jokes around a lot like me, and before long we had a good little banter going. I learned Joe's a doer—he'd rather be doing something than watching something. Best of all, he was sincere about his commitment to honor God with his life. But the whole thing was still a business venture. Could Interstate Batteries gain enough promotion to make the deal worthwhile?

Here's how the deal would work: Joe Gibbs, acting much like the owner of a football team, sells us the right to put our company's name on his players' jerseys. But in motor racing, the player's "jersey" is the exterior of the race car. Interstate, and other sponsors, pay a fee to promote their company name on the car; the bigger the name and the more prominent its placement, the more it costs. The owner uses the money from this advertising to offset his expenses. He takes all the risks, just like any team owner. If Joe's race team does well, he earns more prize and sponsor money, we get more exposure, and everybody is happy. If the team stinks, well . . .

We talked with Joe in great detail face-to-face, and despite his having no NASCAR racing experience, no driver, no crew chief, and no team, our Interstate management group said yes to the deal. We would bank on Joe's history as a "winner" and his ability to choose and get the most out of the men he would select for our team.

As always, trust is a key element in all relationships, both business and personal.

And so began the adventure that led to our big day at the Daytona 500.

The Best Daytona 500 in History

Every race is exciting, but even experienced sportswriters and longtime observers rated the 1993 race as the best Daytona 500 in history. See? I'm not prejudiced!

This race had it all: danger, drama, excitement—everything the 150,000 lucky fans on hand could want. The race produced six wild crashes, all without injury, including a gut-wrenching, barrel-rolling banger of a tangler on lap 169 that sent the Pontiac of Rusty Wallace flipping and rolling eleven times down the backstretch. Amazingly, he walked away from the violent wreck.

On lap 158 of the 200-lap race, Earnhardt made contact with the Chevy of Indianapolis 500 champion Al Unser, Jr. The bump triggered a chain reaction that swept up Bobby Hillin's Ford and Kyle Petty's Pontiac, costing Petty an opportunity to win a $1 million bonus for a Daytona 500 victory put up by his owner, Felix Sabatos.

At lap 174 of the race, Earnhardt was the leader, followed by rookie sensation Jeff Gordon. Dale Jarrett, in the Interstate Batteries car, sped around them both to lead laps 177 and 178. However, he slipped high in turn four of lap 179, allowing Earnhardt and Gordon to whip by on the low side, with Earnhardt again claiming the lead position. Jarrett ran third until the 193rd lap, when he passed Gordon to move into second place.

On lap 198, having noticed that Earnhardt's Lumina was starting to get "loose" or drift in the corners because of the wear on his tires, Jarrett decided to pass him for the lead. He pulled abreast of Earnhardt as lap 199 ended. Entering turn three on the final lap, Jarrett whipped low below Earnhardt—taking the lead—and stayed low coming through turn four. Earnhardt tried bumping Jarrett to upset his momentum as they hurtled toward the finish line.

Up in the CBS booth, Ned Jarrett, Dale's father, himself a two-time NASCAR champion but never a Daytona 500 winner, was handed the mike and told, "Ned, be a father. Root your son home." Finding it impossible to remain objective, especially after seeing Earnhardt's Chevy and his son's Lumina bumping door to door out of turn four and headed toward the checkered flag, Ned began to cheer his son home to victory.

In this, as in all that we try to do through
Interstate Batteries, and in my personal life,
if God isn't in it, I want no part of it.

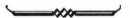

"Come on Dale, go baby go. All right, come on . . . come on, take her to the inside, don't let him get on the inside of you. . . . It's Dale and Dale as they come off turn four. . . . You know who I'm pulling for is Dale Jarrett. . . . Bring her to the inside Dale, don't let him get down there. . . . He's gonna make it, Dale's gonna win the Daytona 500. All right. . . . Oh, can you believe it?!"

Down on pit row with this great victory in hand, pandemonium erupted among the members of the Gibbs/Jarrett/Interstate team. For the last three laps we'd been jumping up and down, cheering, praying, doing everything we could to root Jarrett and our Interstate Batteries Lumina home.

Someone asked me later, "Where were you, Norm, when all this excitement was going on?" Well, I have to tell you about that. I was down in the pit with the radio headset on, listening to the race, but it got so exciting I took it off because we were running second and third and the race was winding down. I could look back to the right and see the cars coming around turn four toward the finish straightaway in front of where we stood. Then they would go into turn one and disappear.

Up behind us in the paddock pavilion, our customers and friends could see our car going all the way around the track. So I watched their faces, to see if anything happened and whether our car was doing okay. When they got really excited, I knew something good was happening. When the car hit turn four, I could see for myself right to the finish line.

Later, I replayed the videos and it was so funny to watch me running around like a chicken with its head cut off! I was spinning around, looking real fast in every direction, trying to find Jimmy Makar, the crew chief. I wanted to be the first to congratulate him—he was the guy in charge of the car and its performance. He, along with Jarrett, had made it happen.

But Joe Gibbs summed up what the rest of us were thinking. After the race he said that the triumph felt just like winning a Super Bowl, but his role was different. "I can't take much credit. My job is to pray and stay out of the way."

God's Stamp of Approval

My son, Scott, was with me at Daytona for that fantastic win. He said this: "It was just an incredible experience, especially when you understand racing and how difficult it is to win. There are forty-two cars, and only one of them wins. In football there are two teams, one wins. The odds of winning at the Daytona 500 are really difficult. When we won the toughest race of the year in our second year of existence, it was unbelievable. Nobody expected us to win. We beat the best driver on the last lap to win. It was like a storybook deal.

"We ran down to the victory lane, and I was there when Dale pulled our car in and got out. There was a full bleacher of photographers taking pictures and it was on the front page of *USA Today* and lots of magazines and newspapers. I was there standing behind Dale and it was so memorable.

"But for my dad, prayer warrior that he is—and he had totally given this to the Lord, and so had Joe Gibbs, Dale, Jimmy Makar, the team players, and all the wives—it was like having God's stamp of approval, and for Dad that was the big thing."

Scott is right. I really felt God's blessing was on the business decision we'd made to sponsor Joe's team. In this, as in all that we try to do through Interstate Batteries, and in my personal life, if God isn't in it, I want no part of it.

That great win reminded me of one of my favorite passages in the Bible: "Now to Him who is able to do exceeding abundantly beyond all that we ask or think, according to the power that works within us" (Eph. 3:20).

Winning the Daytona 500 so soon was certainly "exceeding abundantly" beyond my wildest expectations. Such a success in my life used to make me proud, but now I'm just grateful. That wasn't always the case. For the longest time I thought I had the world by the tail and nothing would stop me from doing just about anything I wanted to. Man, was I wrong about that!

GROWING UP IN GALVESTON

2

My wife says I can talk the tail off a dog. I *do* love to tell stories. Now, I don't always start at the beginning and tell a story straight through. But bear with me, I am headed somewhere with it all.

The story I have to tell in this book is not always a very pretty one, especially not until I met Someone who changed the course I was following with my marriage, my business, and my goals. But I'm not going to try and give you a sales pitch on religion. I simply invite you to listen to my story. It might even be a bit like your own.

Although I was born in Memphis, Tennessee, I spent most of my growing up years around Galveston, Texas. Since the city is surrounded by water, it's no surprise that I became hooked on fishing. In fact, early on in my marriage (I know, I'm jumping ahead in the story, but you've got to trust me!), I probably took my hobby to the extreme. But fishing is fishing!

As newlyweds, my wife, Anne, was determined to get her degree in teaching. And she did, completing college during our first two years of marriage. (My college years are a whole other story, which I'll get to at the right time—maybe?) Then our daughter, Tracey, was born and one day I said, "Anne, I don't want us to get used to living off your salary and mine. Besides, you need to be here at home for the baby."

So in 1967 we decided that after one year of teaching there

was no way Anne was going to continue to work. She quit, and when she received a teachers' retirement fund check for the huge sum (in those days) of $550 in the mail, we were both elated.

I said, "Hey, let's take a trip!"

Anne had other ideas. "We don't even have living room furniture, and I want some dining room furniture too."

Looking back, I'm not sure what my answer says about our marriage or about me, but I responded, "Anne, let me ask you something. When you're eighty years old, sitting in a rocking chair (she was probably wondering, *Will I ever own a rocking chair?*), what are you going to want to look at—some pictures of furniture that you owned or pictures of us vacationing some place like Acapulco?"

Like that beautiful sailfish, I didn't want anybody or anything dictating which way I was going to swim.

My sales pitch must have worked on her, because off we went to Acapulco for a week of what I knew would be a fantastic trip—especially the *fishing*.

Not Just Another Fish Story

One morning down in Mexico Anne woke up with Montezuma's revenge, so, sensitive soul that I was, I felt this would be the best time to try my hand at some local fishing. I wandered down to the boat docks and ran into a guy from Chicago who also wanted to go fishing.

"Do you want to hook up together and rent a boat?" I asked. A boat cost forty dollars a day, so for twenty bucks apiece we headed out to get ourselves some sailfish.

We trolled along offshore for a while when all of a sudden something really *big* hit my line. It was a sailfish! Man, I started setting the hook and holding back. The fight began! (Sailfish often sound first, and then they come up jumping like crazy.) In the middle of my fight with the fish, I noticed that this guy from Chicago was winding *his* rod in, and I thought he was trying to get out of my way because often lines get crossed. My fish was jumping, splashing, and thrashing wildly, trying to throw the hook.

Then my fish came tail walking out of the water again, and I noticed out of the corner of my eye that my partner was still winding like crazy. *Bam!*—another huge fish came out of the water! There were two of them! We both had hooked up at the same time. Unbelievable!

I know it sounds like a "fish" story, but we really landed both of those fighters. Being the competitive sort, I insisted that we measure them both. His fish was bigger than mine—over nine feet long—but not by much. Talk about a memorable experience, and I know Anne will never forget that trip!

Remembering that fish fighting with all his strength and trying to throw the hook reminds me of the way I used to approach life. Like that beautiful sailfish, I didn't want anybody or anything dictating which way I was going to swim. I always thought I could throw the hook. This stubborn independence of mine brought on the toughest fight of my life, one I'm not proud of. But I need to tell about it.

~~~

I must be candid and say that I was a liar and a manipulator when I was young. I was deceitful and lived on the edge—at least from my perspective.

My grades were marginal up through high school and on into five and a half years of college (it takes some of us a bit longer to finish things). I told my teachers and parents anything, whatever I suspected they wanted to hear. I had little respect for anyone in authority. In school it didn't faze me if the principal and teachers liked me or not. I was arrogant and obnoxious. At one point I was even a thief.

My friends and I used to prowl alleys and steal Coke bottles from behind stores—then turn them in again to the same stores for the money. Or, if we'd see stuff in people's backyards that we could sell, we'd go over the fence, steal it, and sell it. We also stole hubcaps.

My most dangerous episode of petty theft happened one night when three of us sneaked into a salvage yard to steal the front doors off a car like mine. My front door windows were cracked, but those on the car in the salvage yard were in perfect condition. It seemed daring at the time—fearlessly going after what I wanted. Now I see it as foolish and incredibly stupid!

One of my cohorts, Hans, was Dutch. The other was a Mexican buddy, Rudy. We crawled around in the salvage yard on our bellies, like we were Marines on the front lines. There weren't any guard dogs, but all of a sudden searchlights flashed on and someone started shooting. A bullet ricocheted off one of the cars and got Rudy in the knee. In minutes both he and Hans were caught, but I crawled under a wooden flatbed off an old truck. I told myself to be still and even tried to go to sleep so I wouldn't move. I didn't fall asleep, but I did wait until all was quiet and I was sure everyone was gone. I slithered out and sneaked away. Hans and Rudy were my good buddies and didn't implicate me.

When I've told that story to some people, they've reacted incredulously: "Why did you do that? Did you need the money?"

The answer is: I was a smart-aleck sixteen-year-old. I wanted those car doors for free. I didn't need the money; I had a good job. But it showed my total disregard for what others thought and felt. At that juncture in my life I had no values and my only priorities were to do what Bubba (my nickname) wanted to do—regardless of the consequences to others or myself.

I figured I was smart enough to outwit the odds and things would come my way. No matter what happened, I could always spit out the hook.

Growing Up on "The Island"

I was not quite five years old when my family moved from Houston to Galveston. In 1943 Galveston was a bustling, bawdy war town, a port of 95,000 with a long-standing, well-deserved reputation for drinking, partying, gambling, and prostitution. Galvestonians have always called it "the Island," with the city being joined to the mainland by a three-mile-long umbilical causeway, now a part of Interstate 45 from Houston. The island is three miles wide and thirty-five miles long.

Growing up with a diverse mix of people really
helped me learn to relate and be at ease with
all types of people.

My father had purchased a Gulf Oil service station and garage right in the middle of Galveston. It was during World War II, and servicemen swarmed everywhere, especially guys in the Navy and the Coast Guard.

As a child I heard all the stories about Galveston's glory days. I learned about the "Great Storm" of September 8, 1900, when a hurricane and tidal wave covered the island in water from gulf to bay, killing an estimated six thousand people and drowning much of the city's prosperity until World War I.

Every schoolboy's favorite Galveston story, though, had to do with the pirate Jean Lafitte, a handsome, dashing renegade who, along with another man passing himself off as Lafitte's brother, engaged in piracy and smuggling, while ostensibly posing as entrepreneurs operating a blacksmith shop. Lafitte declared himself to be a privateer, not a pirate, who knew the best, the richest, and the most interesting people. He mingled with planters, traders, and merchants with their bejeweled ladies outfitted in low-cut gowns, and he provided them with a dazzling array of desired merchandise—furs, linens, silver, jewelry, cinnamon, black ivory, and slaves.

Stories abounded about this rebel who set fire to Galveston one spring night in 1821 and sailed away forever. Nobody knows what happened to Jean Lafitte who, at one time, was even appointed governor of the Island—a man who it is said talked out of both sides of his mouth, looted ships, then loved to come back to port and party.

I soaked up all these stories of adventure. And as an imaginative kid, I was influenced by all the excitement and glamour of a party town like Galveston, with open gambling, liquor by the drink twenty-four hours a day, and houses of prostitution lining several blocks. All of this was controlled by a local crime family and, of course, was in violation of state and federal laws. It wasn't the most wholesome place to raise a family, to say the least, but today Balveston is a wonderful, family-driven beach resort and historical destination.

My father's four-bay service station and garage, coupled with the way he took care of his customers, earned him the respect of the business community. Twice he was elected president of the Texas Service Station Association. But Dad had a problem—one that would later be my problem too.

From all appearances, we had a reasonably normal middle-class family. Besides Mom and Dad, there were four kids: my older brother, Jim, my sister, Janet, then me, and my younger brother Tommy. We lived in a quiet, well-kept frame house in a nice neighborhood, which was uniquely Galvestonian in that it was in close proximity to different ethnic groups in a lower income neighborhood one street over.

We played football and baseball with the other kids, especially on Saturdays, down at the school a block away. Color or station in life didn't matter; winning was the goal. Growing up with a diverse mix of people really helped me learn to relate and be at ease with all types of people.

My passion for fishing I owe to the influence of my mother's brother, ol' Uncle Tom, who loved to fish and was always taking me with him. During the summer my mom would pack a lunch for me and off I'd go. I had to get up at 5:10 A.M., catch a bus that ran near our home, then transfer to another bus and get down to what was called "The Pleasure Pier." It was a long concrete and reinforced-metal pier, eight or ten blocks long, with a fishing T-head at the end about fifteen to eighteen feet above the water.

I became infatuated with watching the old men casting with their long rods and large reels. For bait they used live fish that were over a foot long! These old guys were out to hook the tarpon, the premier sport fish of the world, and they used corks the size of pineapples. These marvelous game fish, when hooked, come up out of the water six to eight feet, with great big gills and giant mouths.

Man, when I saw one of those, would I get excited. But there I was, my line dangling in the water, with some dead shrimp for bait. I wondered if I would ever get to fish for the big ones like those guys.

～～～

My younger brother, Tommy, and I had the usual brotherly fights when we were kids. Of course, being five years older definitely worked to my advantage. Because of Uncle Tom, Tommy was called "Little Tommy." Today "Little Tommy" is over six feet three inches tall, just like our dad.

Tommy reminds me every chance he gets that I was always extremely energetic and, in his words, "creative." He claims that we couldn't sit together on the curb waiting for a bus for ten minutes before I'd start a game. This restless spirit was a driving force within me in my childhood, and I was always looking for a good time. Unfortunately, when I was still very young, alcohol became a part of the fun.

Like Father, Like Son

My father was a heavy drinker for many years, although he went "on the wagon" when I was about eight. He remained a recovering alcoholic the rest of his life. I decided to follow in his footsteps—the drinking, not the recovering part.

I was only fourteen when I started drinking "for fun." Partying, drinking, and having a good time—that became my major game plan in life, so I gravitated toward the people who had the same goal. Of course, this was easy to do in Galveston, one great big party town.

Back when my father was drinking, every Saturday afternoon around two o'clock, he and others at his service station would set up a little bar in a back room, and regular customers had a standing invitation to go on back.

My father serviced a lot of big fleet accounts such as the telephone company. Having the location that he did, and being the entrepreneur he was, he went after bigger and bigger commercial accounts. And they would come by to pay their bills on Saturday afternoon. He excused all this back room drinking by saying he just wanted to have a little fun and, besides, it was good for business.

Partying, drinking, and having a good time—that became my major game plan in life.

I remember him often coming home drunk and my mother being furious at his condition, as well as his being late. Sometimes his buddies or employees would have to bring him home because he was so drunk he had passed out. They would have to carry him to bed. Mother would yell and scream and sometimes even hit him. This environment for us kids left a lot to be desired in many ways, but we loved our folks, and they loved us too.

In respect to his business habits, though, my father was a good role model for me. He was an excellent salesman, and his service station was like a community general automotive store. No doubt my interest in cars and the automotive business hatched here. These were in the days before Chief Auto Parts, Western Auto, and other big chains. Dad stocked not only tires and batteries and automotive repair parts, but also tailpipes, chrome tailpipe extenders, mirrors, seat covers—everything needed to turn an ordinary car into a prized machine.

From early on, selling and serving the customer have always been important to me, and I owe a lot of that to the influence of my father.

❧

When I was just fifteen, I got my first real job at the Balinese Room, an elite, private, illegal gambling casino and nightclub. This employment fit well into my "life's a party" outlook.

A friend's father owned a piece of the Balinese. It was considered the swankiest and most famous nightspot in all of Texas. The decor was South Seas, with everything made to look like some exotic tropical island paradise.

The supper club/casino was located on Seawall Boulevard, an impressive ocean drive right next to the beach. From the 1920s to the mid-1950s, this boulevard was a glittering strip of hotels, nightclubs, and boardwalks. The Balinese Room extended two thousand feet out over the gulf at the foot of 21st Street. It had acquired the reputation of hosting the biggest names of the day in show business—Peggy Lee, Freddy Martin, Ray Noble, Shep Fields, Jimmy Dorsey, Joe E. Lewis, Sophie Tucker, Joey Bishop, Rowan and Martin, and on and on. For a young guy of fifteen with partying on his mind, it was a once-in-a-life-time experience to work at the famed club.

The Balinese hosted some of the highest-rolling gamblers in America. It was next to impossible to raid because the casino area, where all the illegal activity took place, was located far out on the gulf end of the pier. If the Texas Rangers appeared unexpectedly, someone at the front of the pier pushed a button that sounded an alarm in the back. The band would strike up "The Eyes of Texas" and, incredibly, the gambling paraphernalia would fold into the walls and the green felt-covered crap tables would convert instantly into pool, backgammon, and bridge tables. As it was, the owners were usually tipped in advance when a raid was planned anyway. "Payola" was the name of the game in those days.

All of this made quite an impression on my adolescent mind and helped to pave the way for future problems. Yet, up until I was fifteen,

I attended church with my family. As a kid I won awards for good Sunday school attendance and for memorizing Bible verses, but going to church never went very deep for me.

Reflecting on my early years, I can see where there was little spiritual influence in the home. I mention this only as a detail of my background, not as an excuse for my behavior as I grew into adulthood.

If it's true that I'm a creative person, I must have inherited much of that quality from my mother. She was free-spirited and all my friends loved her. As teenagers we called her by her first name, Ruth. She was five feet and two inches tall with eyes of blue and about 140 pounds. Mom was great for hugging on!

Mom was fun, unpredictable, a risk taker, and at times quite an entrepreneur. I remember when Galveston passed a law that said you could no longer set your garbage on the street in bags and boxes. From now on, the trash had to be in cans. Mom said to Dad, "You need to go to Houston and buy a bunch of trash cans. You could stack them sky-high in front of the service station and with all the traffic going by, you'll sell a bunch."

As a kid I won awards for good Sunday school attendance and for memorizing Bible verses, but going to church never went very deep for me.

"I run a service station," Daddy said. "I don't want cars blocking my driveway. We'll lose money on all this. I'm not in the garbage can business."

My mom wouldn't let it go. She recruited Dad's brother to help, and they convinced my father to let them sell trash cans at the service station. They sold like crazy! I guess I learned some things about taking risks and being willing to try "wild ideas" from her.

In spite of the alcoholism, Mom loved my dad very much. He was a big man—six feet four inches—and had a dark moustache and thick, black hair. He was a fun-loving guy and great at telling jokes. My friends called him Mr. Miller for a while, but as with my mom, that eventually changed to Lawrence.

My family was certainly wounded somewhat, but we hung in there. We were and still are a family. My parents held together and held us together, and I respect and love them for that. Today's society is paying a dear price for that lack of responsibility and committed love in marriages and families.

Time moved on, and like the legendary Lafitte, I left Galveston behind me one day. I took with me that bent to party that nearly ruined my life. Any old port will do when you're out to party and have what you think is fun, but I don't recommend the way I chose. I was just running, fighting my way through life against a better way to live.

LEAVING HOME

3

As a senior in high school, I was even more free to pursue my self-centered, wild, life-of-the-party ways. That last year at home I mostly called my own shots and did what I pleased. My parents just held on and hoped for the best. I paid little attention to them.

That Christmas my Aunt "Doots" and Uncle "Pistol" from Louisiana were visiting with us for the holidays. Doots and my mom were talking in the kitchen one evening as I was heading out to party somewhere. As I got to the car, I realized I'd forgotten something and went back in the house. Mom and Doots didn't hear me return, but I overheard them.

"Where's Bubba going to college?" I heard Doots ask Mom.

"College? Heck, I just hope we can keep him out of jail and get him out of high school!"

That pretty much sums up the road I was traveling.

One of my best friends, Tony Fertitta, had attended North Texas State (NTS) in Denton, and one day he suggested to a buddy and me that we should write for applications. I hadn't given college much thought, but I had heard it could be a big party experience. We saw ourselves as "rock-'em-up-good-time-guys" out to meet some party gals and have ourselves a good time! So I enrolled at NTS.

Business, Booze, and the Hi-Low Club

One day four of us fraternity brothers were bemoaning the fact that we were flat broke. Getting jobs never seemed to enter our discussion. We just wanted some quick, easy money. So we hit on the idea of starting a private club to bootleg liquor into dry Denton County.

Being the business tycoons that we were, we decided that first we had to come up with a catchy name. The Hi-Low Club was our pick. Next, we printed up four hundred membership cards, with two cards for each member. Out we went to sign up fellow partyers. Memberships sold for a buck apiece, and we only sold to people we knew. Members signed both cards; they got one, and we kept one. We filed the halves we kept alphabetically, and the Hi-Low Club was ready to go operational.

I wish I could say that by this time I had grown up a little and learned some lessons. Not me.

The two hundred dollars from membership fees was seed money, our working capital that enabled us to buy the inventory for our venture. We didn't want to use our real names, so we opened a checking account under a pseudonym and actually got away with it. Hey, we were smooth operators, and nothing could stop us!

With cash in hand we headed for Dallas, and when we hit a "wet" area (where it was legal to buy liquor), we made a deal to purchase the stuff at a volume discount. We brought the booze back to Denton and opened for business.

The Hi-Low Club was a hit, a huge success. In fact, we got to the point where we were doing so much business out of our small house that we had to hire other guys to help sell. At one point we were moving fifteen to twenty cases of beer a day and three or four cases of whiskey a week, with sales really booming on the weekends.

The traffic began to cause a problem in the neighborhood, so we knew we had to relocate. We found some fellows who had rented a house on a big corner lot. Big operators that we now were, we made a deal to pay their rent, and they agreed to work all the shifts. It got to the point where we were so busy with this arrangement that the club was open until eleven at night. Then we'd lock up and do an inventory.

Every Monday it was back to Dallas to restock. This went on for nine profitable months until we got word that we'd better stop or we'd be in big trouble. Some people in Denton had complained, and the sheriff told a friend to tell us that our little business was over.

Did that stop us? Nah, it only made us become more creative. We decided to have rock 'n' roll dances at the National Guard Armory. We rented the building on Thursdays and brought in bands. Thursday was a slack day at college, so we were able to start the parties about one in the afternoon and go until ten at night—ending just in time for the girls to make it back to their dorms by the 10:50 curfew.

We would buy eight to ten kegs of draft beer, and a friend would load them into a small trailer that he towed behind his car. We'd pull the car and trailer right into the armory and sell from there. Some other friends who worked at a funeral home had a radio scanner that let them listen in to police reports. If they heard anything heading our way, they would call right away. We'd raise the door, drive the car and the trailer with the kegs out, and there was never a problem.

We charged a couple of bucks a head and twenty-five cents a cup for beer and made good money. I rationalized the whole thing by telling myself that students were gonna party anyway, and this way we were keeping them off the highways to Dallas or Fort Worth to party.

This venture also came to an end, mainly because it became too much work. With four to five hundred people coming and going and the logistics of getting the bands, selling the beer, and keeping track of the cash, we realized we had inadvertently stumbled into the hard work of running a business. Remember, we had wanted to party and make *easy* money. So we hung it up.

I wish I could say that by this time I had grown up a little and learned some lessons. Not me. I'm a lot more stubborn than that. We drank up a lot of the profit from our business. Many was the time my friend Tony had to take care of me, hoisting me over his shoulder, hauling me to the apartment, and dumping me in bed.

Looking back, I ask myself, "And you called that fun?" The continual drinking and dependence on alcohol made me wilder and more belligerent. I'm fortunate I had friends looking out for me.

〜〜〜

As you can probably guess, running the business and being drunk half the time caused my college class work to suffer. My grades nose-dived, but I wasn't exactly in college to refine my mind anyway. Our fraternity was considered a hard drinking, rough party bunch—mavericks set on doing our own thing. The saddest part of all this was that I thought I had it all together and was on track for a great life. I was on track all right, but my bad habits were like a train roaring head-on toward me from the opposite direction. I was out of touch with reality.

Wake-Up Call: "Hit the Road!"

I did get some wake-up calls now and then, though, while working for my dad during the summer months. Dad had a pretty big service station going by now, and he would put me on one of the crews during the summers, working different shifts. I serviced cars, pumped gas, and checked oil, as well as performing general care and maintenance.

My shift started at eight in the morning, but I was often out drinking and partying until the wee hours of the morning. I remember walking out of some of the best of Galveston's clubs at daybreak! That doesn't give a man much time to sober up, rest, and get to work by eight.

One morning in the summer of 1958, after my sophomore year, my dad woke me up. I had a really awful hangover. I mumbled to him, "I've been thinking. I'll come in at one so I can work until ten tonight."

"Son, I don't need you from one to ten. I've got you on a crew, and I need you from eight to six."

"Well, I can't make it," I said as I fell back on the bed.

"Let me put it to you this way, son. You either make it or just pack your stuff and hit the road before I get home tonight!"

Tough and stubborn me, always ready to bluff my way through, and with an alcohol-fogged mind, replied, "If that's the way you want it, Pop, you got it!"

My father stormed out of my room, and I lay there, proud of my know-it-all attitude. *Who does he think he is? I don't need this,* I thought to myself. *Why mess with this junk and put up with all this garbage?* I was mad and itching to get away from home anyway, to get out on my own. But then another thought struck me: *Hey, I'm twenty years old. Where am I going? What am I gonna do with my life?*

I lay there with my head pounding and my stomach turning over and over. Reality set in and I thought, *If I'm not in college anymore, I won't have a college deferment, and they will draft me into the army.* (And I definitely *did not* want to go into the army.) *That means if I don't go to college, then all these guys who are going to college will end up with a degree. And when I get out of the army, what will I have? Nothing. Their degrees will open doors for jobs that I won't even be able to apply for. I'm not cut out for army life anyway.* All of a sudden my hit-the-road-leave-home choice wasn't so appealing!

In my room there was a little closet, with a clothes rod on two sides and about a foot and a half space in the middle between them. My momma had stored some suitcases on the floor. Somewhere in the middle of all this high-powered thinking that I was doing, I went into the closet to get out a suitcase. After all, I was getting ready to leave.

Hung over, with no sleep, I pulled up a suitcase, sat down on it, and contemplated my life. My rear end was covered by clothes hanging on one side of the closet, and my face was buried in another row of clothes on the other side. There I was, sitting in a dark, stuffy closet, doing some of the most crucial thinking I'd ever done in my life. It's a picture I've never forgotten.

I made my decision. I pulled on my Gulf Tire and Supply Company uniform and headed for the bus stop and Dad's station. How different my life might have been if I had played out that hand any other way. Like I've said before, I was still trying to throw that hook, but Someone on the other end wasn't giving up on me!

My confusing life was about to become even more confusing. A pretty Texas girl can do that to a guy.

What was funny (and I can still remember the day as if it were yesterday) was my less than triumphant return to my dad's service station. Located on the corner of a big intersection, the station had pumps on both sides so we could serve customers coming from either street. The station was built so that the front door pointed directly toward the street corner so you could watch both sides through the station's big windows.

My dad smoked, and he would come out and stand right in front where he could watch everything that was going on. He'd take a final drag off his cigarette, pitch it out, go back in, sit down, and see what was happening inside the station. Then he'd light another cigarette only moments later, come out, and walk around again. The driveway bells constantly rang as the cars came and went.

The bus let me off a half block away from the station. I hiked right up there, arriving just as a car was pulling up. Without even breaking my stride, I jumped right in helping the guys service the car. I checked the oil and the battery, swept out the car, put in some gas, and cleaned the windows. Out of the corner of my eye I saw my dad come out, take a big drag off his cigarette, look both ways, throw the smoke away, and go back inside. I heaved a sigh of relief and decided everything was going to be all right.

That fall I went back to college.

A Pretty Texas Girl

I'd like to be able to tell you that things took off from there, and that I was on the straight and true from that point on; but I was still partying, going down the only road I really knew. My confusing life was about to become even more confusing. A pretty Texas girl can do that to a guy.

I was attending summer school (trying to catch up a little and wondering if I would ever get out of college) when I first met Anne on a waterskiing outing at Lake Dallas. Later that evening, the guys asked the gals to go out and party, and Anne and I ended up as dates. I learned that she was from Galveston, too, but we'd never met before. Anne only attended school the first part of that summer, and just as our relationship was beginning to blossom, she left and returned home. I stayed in Denton, but it was tough, especially now that I was lonely for Anne.

At the end of the summer a few of my buddies got married and I was in their weddings. After that, I decided to hitchhike home. One of the guys dropped me off at a well-known traffic circle in Dallas. I was headed for Galveston and Anne.

For some reason, however, as I sat there on the roadside on my suitcase (back then, I seemed to do some of my best thinking while sitting on a suitcase!), those old demon doubts started to play with my mind. I remember thinking, *Why am I going home? Well, I just got things going with Anne, and if I don't go home, I can probably forget that relationship. But, on the other hand, I could go to Las Vegas and see a friend, and maybe get a job out there as a dealer. I'd like to blow this whole school deal off, once and for all. I'm tired of it. I could use some fun.*

I pondered my choices for a few minutes, before saying to myself, "Okay, tell you what I'm going to do. I'm going to hitchhike for thirty minutes, and if I get a ride toward Vegas, then that's what I'm going to do. If I don't, I'm going home."

The future stretched before me. The way I was headed, my life didn't hold much promise. I had few goals; time was only something to be used to satisfy myself. My actions were primarily a disgrace to my hardworking parents. I was a poor example for my younger brother.

And I had to admit that the most important priorities in my life were partying, having a good time, and drinking.

Myron Rush wrote: "Priorities are the 'guardrails' on the road of life, they keep us on track. They also keep us from getting bogged down in the mire of ineffectiveness. How far and how fast you travel in life will depend on how faithful you are at developing and maintaining your priorities."[1]

I desperately needed guardrails. I was on a fast track, but I didn't know where it was headed. I can't remember if I really waited thirty minutes that day at the traffic circle or not. I *did* move across the circle with my thumb stuck out to the roads headin' west, away from Galveston. Although many cars whizzed by, none of those heading west stopped to offer me a ride. My feeble effort at making a decisive choice fizzled. Aimlessly, I ended up going south, home to Galveston.

Back on the island I resumed seeing Anne. I was four years older, and I seemed mature and worldly to her. I impressed her with my carefree confidence and wild ways. After all, Anne was a dyed-in-the-wool Galveston girl who had rarely ever stepped foot off the island.

I got her interested in drinking and partying, taking her to all the rockin' spots in Dallas and dancing the night away. I could tell she liked my take-charge attitude as well as my love of a good time, and I treated her with respect and politeness. She once told me she saw me as sophisticated because I showed an interest in the world at large, reading the newspaper from cover to cover "just like her dad."

Since I was about to graduate from college, I was thinking more about marriage and the qualities I would want in a wife. Like so many guys, what I wanted in a bride was a bit different from what I'd been looking for during my "let's party" days. Anne definitely fit the bill. She was beautiful, and I liked her quiet, gracious ways. She had grown up in a modest home and knew the value of a dollar. Yet she dressed well. I also liked the fact that she seemed so down-to-earth.

I probably sensed that I would need somebody who kept at least one foot on the ground. On just our second date, I had taken her to

Dallas to go dancing. I got half lit, and on the way home, I told her—as seriously as I could in my condition—that I thought I probably was going to marry her. She just laughed.

When my father sold his Galveston service station, he asked me to join him in opening an automotive battery distributorship for Interstate Batteries in Memphis.

During this summer romance in 1961, Hurricane Carla smashed into Galveston. Having both been raised on the island, Anne and I had each experienced many storms, but nothing quite like Carla. The whole city was encouraged to evacuate, so I drove my parents across the causeway to the mainland. I left them in Houston, and drove back to be with Anne. Anne's family had elected to stay, just because that's what they always did in storms. They took all the usual precautions but were eventually forced out of their home to higher ground. I caught up with them at the Jack Tar Hotel, where they were holed up. The city was under martial law.

I volunteered to work with Civil Defense so I could travel around at night. You can imagine Anne's father's delight when I showed up each evening—all the lights out on the island, Anne and I sitting in the darkened room at the Jack Tar on the sofa while he loomed somewhere in the shadows.

Anne and I stayed in Galveston to help clean up after the hurricane, so we both got back to college a bit late that fall. By then we were dating steadily. I finally graduated that December and returned to Galveston where I ended up selling encyclopedias.

Knocking on doors and selling books was not exactly the career I had envisioned while in college, but a venture my father and I had planned didn't come together, so door-to-door I went. When my father sold his Galveston service station, he asked me to join him in opening an automotive battery distributorship for Interstate Batteries in Memphis.

Interstate, as a national company, was in its second year of seeking to develop a national system of battery distributors. With its home office in Dallas, business was good and national expansion looked encouraging.

I was single and pretty highly motivated by this time. Of course, Anne was very much on my mind. She had left college to train as an airline stewardess. She started flying all over the country. I got a little nervous and decided in the summer of 1962 it was time to get a ring on her finger. The strange thing is that I didn't have any part in picking it out; a friend of mine selected it and brought it to Anne because he could get it wholesale. (I always save a buck if I can!)

We began planning to marry in December and started to save our money so our parents would not have to pay for the wedding. There was only one little interruption to our plans, however. The world knows it as the Cuban Missile Crisis. Let me explain.

Sitting Out the Cuban Missile Crisis

Back in the sixties, without a college deferment, you got drafted into the military. Bad grades had canceled my deferment, so instead of allowing myself to get drafted for a two-year stint, I joined the Air Force Reserve, which required only six months of active duty, five and a half years of meetings one weekend per month, and a two-week summer camp each year. Through the Air Force Reserve, I missed just one semester of school, avoided a two-year potluck assignment in the army, and had a choice of career training. Also, all of my active duty was spent in Texas—San Antonio and Dallas.

Three months before our wedding date, I was watching television one Saturday night. President Kennedy came on the air to say the United States was getting ready to call up the Air Force Reserve troops. Guess who was in the Air Force Reserve!

I'd just transferred from a reserve unit in Texas to one in Tennessee. All the other men in my new unit were from the Midsouth and were already good buddies. And I wasn't getting too well acquainted because of my unique way of "serving."

When I transferred from Dallas, I had reported to headquarters in Memphis, but never visibly to my unit. When it came time for weekend active duty, I'd go into my unit wearing my uniform, mix in the crowd, sign the pay roster, and then immediately slide right out unnoticed.

I just never bothered to report in person to anyone in my unit! After signing in I'd go straight to the commissary for breakfast, then to the library, read the newspaper, or watch a ball game. When duty was over, I'd head home. None of the eighty or so guys knew who I was!

It caught up with me that Saturday when the president spoke. Bang! By nine o'clock that night, my group was activated. At our first muster for the Cuban Crisis, the captain walked out and then the sergeant started calling names. I heard, "Airman Miller . . . Norman Miller . . . Miller, where are you? I'd like to know what you look like. Come up here, we'd all like to look at you. Our records show you've been attending here for three months, but nobody's laid eyes on you!" If you have ever served in the armed forces, you can just imagine the tone of voice this sergeant was using! I knew my time was up.

I was assigned to what they called "Roads and Grounds" since I was a heavy-duty construction equipment operator apprentice (how's that for a short and sweet bureaucratic title?). I'd been trained to operate road and construction equipment, except they didn't have any equipment. Nothing but a garbage truck.

"Now, since we only have one garbage truck," explained the sergeant, "and there are ten of us, what we're going to do is rotate on and off the truck each day. We'll rotate everybody through."

That sounded fair enough to me, so the first day there were four of us—a driver and a rider with him, and two guys on the back haulin' in the garbage. I was one of those on the back of the truck, and off we went to pick up the day's garbage.

The next day they announced the crew change. Three names changed, except for mine, and I'm once again on the back ridin' with the flies. On the third day they rotated again, except for—you guessed it—I'm hanging on the back. I was getting the picture. That sergeant had a long memory, I suppose.

I spent the next twenty-seven days of the Cuban Crisis defending my country by playing poker.

Anyway, I asked myself, "Norm, what are you going to do now?" The plan I came up with was to work as fast as I could, to be the Charlie Hustle of garbage detail. I obnoxiously urged the other workers to do the same. Rush, rush, rush; move it, move it, move it! And I kept talking the whole time. "Hey, come on! Let's go! Roll that truck! Move it out!"

All the time I was literally running from place to place, and subsequently the others had to do the same. But my plan was to be so annoying they'd *want* me off the truck "team." I even coined a little song when I'd hit the offices of the officers to empty their wastebaskets: "I'm Norman E. Miller, your refuse man; I empty your trash and garbage cans. Have you any trash for me today?"

Well, after three days they kicked me off the crew.

But the Cuban Crisis was still on, meaning we were still on active duty. So after not bonding in "Roads and Grounds," they transferred me to the fire department. Guess how many fire trucks we had? Nada. None.

I spent the next twenty-seven days of the Cuban Crisis defending my country by playing poker. In November we were deactivated, and I returned to working for my dad in Memphis.

On December 29, 1962, Anne and I were married. The proverbial "small" wedding we planned grew to about three hundred guests. We got married in a Presbyterian church still decorated for Christmas.

Our honeymoon was short but sweet. We left the church and headed for Hot Springs, Arkansas, known at the time as "the little Las Vegas of the South." We drove as far as Livingston, Texas, and since

I hadn't made reservations anywhere until our final destination, found the only motel in town with an available room. Unfortunately, it was an unfinished room. So our first night as Mr. and Mrs. Norm Miller was spent in a half-finished room.

Looking back, maybe that room was a sign of how far we would have to travel in the years ahead to build a complete, solid marriage that would honor the vows we'd made to each other and to God.

PARTY TIME

4

After our honeymoon, we settled down in Memphis in a furnished duplex that rented for seventy-five dollars a month. My salary was ninety dollars a week, and Anne worked as a bank teller for two hundred a month. We decided to put Anne's earnings aside so she could eventually go back to college.

My family lived less than a mile away, and Anne spent many happy times over there getting to know my parents and my brothers, Jimmy and Tommy, who were working for Dad now as well. Anne loved my family. But it was me that she had married, and I was out of town a lot, working hard, to be sure, but depending more and more on alcohol to fill a void. I told myself I drank to help me relax and handle the pressures. In truth, alcohol was taking over my life.

Anne says that even in the first year of our marriage there were shadows looming in the background beginning to show the patterns of my drinking. Once a month I had to go do my weekend of Air Force Reserve duty. We drank and partied most of those weekends. Anne was getting a taste of what it was like to have a husband more interested in drinking with his buddies than in being with her.

Anne's family had taught her what commitment in marriage meant. They came from the generation that taught that couples could work through anything that came along. Besides, between my drinking bouts, things were going well, and we even partied together sometimes. Anne says that she tried to view my behavior as an occasional problem when things simply got a little out of control.

Like I said, we had a lot of fun times too. Anne returned to school, and we moved to a new apartment complex that was, of all places, right across the street from Elvis's Graceland. About the same time we bought a ski boat with my brother Tommy. All of us loved to ski, and Anne was great at it. We spent many weekends camping out and using the boat. Even on weekdays we frequently took the boat out after work and skied on the Mississippi River.

We didn't have a lot of money, so we made our fun where we could find it. We hardly ever went to the movies and never went out to eat, but we spent a lot of time with the rest of my family, getting together often for potluck dinners.

Things began to change, however. Anne became pregnant in February of 1964. Then my mother, Ruth, died unexpectedly in August of a heart attack at the age of fifty-six. It was hard to believe that she was gone. My brothers and I spent the whole night at the funeral home, unable to pull ourselves away from Mom.

Anne and I soon found out about all the joys and heartaches of being parents ourselves when our daughter, Tracey, was born in November of 1964. Parenthood is a humbling experience that can bring incredible highs and unbelievable lows. I regret now that much of my parenting in those early years had to compete with my partying and business travel.

We prepared to move to Dallas. John Searcy, the founder and president of Interstate Batteries, had offered me an opportunity at the national office that was too good to turn down. The move from Memphis was made in short order, and then began several years of my traveling most of the time, spending the weeks on the road building up Interstate, and, of course, when I was at home, drinking much of the time with my ol' North Texas buddies.

In 1966 Anne returned to Memphis for six weeks to fulfill her student teaching requirement. I know it was difficult for her, but she was determined to get that degree to be true to the promise she had made to her father. She lived with my brothers and their wives and put Tracey in day care.

I regret now that so much of my parenting in those early years had to compete with my partying and business travel.

I think the reality of my problem really hit her on one occasion while she was in Memphis. It was a clue to the heartache to come. She was staying with Jimmy and Jean when she heard the phone ring in their bedroom late one night. A few minutes later she heard it again and went to stand at the door to listen. She suspected the worst. A chill went up her spine when she heard Jimmy say, "What? You're in jail?" I had been arrested for "walking while intoxicated." I ended up calling a friend, and he came down and bailed me out in the wee hours of the morning.

Anne and I worked hard at keeping appearances normal, though. In June of 1968, we were blessed with the birth of our son, Scott. We bought a three-bedroom house in Dallas, which we never did completely furnish. The living and dining rooms became the places where the kids played most of the time, since those rooms were empty.

The pattern of drinking continued as I started stopping at bars on the way home from work to "turn off my brain." It then progressed to not coming home until two or three in the morning. We were two struggling people trying to make a go of our relationship. It wasn't until we were well into our tenth year of marriage that we came to understand our problems and how they were affecting us individually—me, the alcoholic, and her, the enabler. I had more and more pressures at work and used alcohol out of habit to self-medicate myself. Things began to boil over.

The Old Family Pattern

My accomplishments at Interstate were great, but behind the scenes at home, the problems festered and grew. Our disagreements were usually over the children and how to discipline them.

We each went through our own established pattern. I would stay out, party, and come home drunk, which would drive Anne up the wall. Then we would reconcile and everything would be hunky-dory until the next episode. This emotional seesaw is what our children felt while they were growing up.

Finally, it got to the point where I wouldn't even call to tell Anne I would be late because I didn't feel like getting into another confrontation over my behavior. Anne would have dinner on the table, doing her best to run the house with two little kids under her feet. She wanted to make everything just right for me, like *Leave It to Beaver*'s June Cleaver, but then, once again, I wouldn't show up at all.

Our son, Scott, remembers Anne and I having some real knock-down-drag-out fights. I had a real controlling type of personality. And to top it off, I had a bad temper that I easily lost control of.

Despite the troubles Anne and I were having, I was a caring father. The kids still talk about the fun times we had, and still have as a family. I coached soccer and enjoyed being a teacher and companion to the children and their friends.

But all the good works and fun didn't make up for the selfish sin of my alcoholic behavior. I know that our children lived with a cloud of tension around them that could have been cut with a knife. Anne puts a share of the blame on herself for not being more constructively confrontational and direct in dealing with me.

I'd been getting loaded at least once a week for twenty years, often drinking to the point of blacking out. I still find it amazing to think that I was able to win the respect and affection of John Searcy and help grow Interstate in those earlier years. The drinking never affected my work, as far as I could tell. My family was falling apart around me, but I was too busy partying and building my exciting new career, being groomed for top management, to notice.

Being on the road so much didn't help my drinking problem. Often we traveled in teams, and we would be gone from Sunday afternoon until Friday night. Although there's nothing wrong with football, when ABC-TV started televising *Monday Night Football,* that gave us road warriors another good reason to drink. If we were out West, the game would come on relatively early, so we would just skip dinner. We'd meet in someone's room to eat snacks and drink. On an empty stomach, it often didn't take long before we lost interest in the game and headed out to the bars.

Fridays were the worst, though. I would always drink and party on the plane ride home. In fact, once I'd had two or three drinks, I wanted to keep going until everything shut down and the bottle was empty. Later I'd feel badly about it, but drinking seemed to ease a pressure that would build up in me every four or five days.

Anne had decided that sooner or later she was going to leave me, for her own sake as well as that of our children. She was familiar with what alcohol could do to relationships. She got to the point, the courageous point, where she said to herself, "This is not going to change; it's getting worse and I've got to get out of this situation." She called several school districts to find out if she could go back to teaching, and she checked out some apartments.

Incredibly, my abuse of alcohol worsened. As time went on, in classic alcoholic behavior, I needed more and more booze to be satisfied. I also developed the habit of drinking before I went to sleep. I would pour myself two large drinks, often draining the last one as I lay in bed with the lights off.

One night in March 1974, after working late, I stopped at a friend's bar in Dallas. I had consciously made the decision that I did not want to get drunk. That was specifically not my intention. I just was not going to do it. But one round led to another, and I ended up drinking as usual until the bar closed at two in the morning. Afterward, as I was driving home, I got pulled over by the police. I already had two DWI convictions, but I lied my way out of getting arrested.

I had asked a friend who was a car salesman in Memphis,

Tennessee, to find a car for Anne, which I happened to be driving that night. Some months before this, when Texas had suspended my driver's license because of my two DWIs, I'd gone up to Memphis and lied in order to get another driver's license. I had to have a license to rent cars for business travel. I told the Tennessee driver's license people that I'd been in England for five years, and my driver's license had lapsed but I wanted to renew it. They told me I was over the deadline time limit, and I would have to take the driving test again. "Please, I'm busy, I've got to go to New York today," I argued, and they gave in and issued me a license.

Anne had decided that sooner or later she was going to leave me, for her own sake as well as that of our children.

Now here I was pulled over on Central Expressway in Dallas; it's about 2:30 A.M., and a big ol' policeman is asking for my license. He notices that I have Tennessee tags on the car, with a Tennessee driver's license. I lied again and told him that I'd just moved to Dallas, so he didn't even check the Texas records. I was so convincing that one of the policemen drove me home in the police car, and the other drove my car. They were giving a "new resident" of Texas a break, unaware that I had no business being out on the road at all.

When I woke up the next morning all hung over, I called the office and lied, telling them I was too sick to work. Then, as I lay there in bed, the truth started to overwhelm me. Although on the outside I represented the ultimate on the American success track—great job, lots of money, pretty wife, cute kids, fancy car—in reality I was a drunk. My life was out of control. The realization scared me like nothing else ever had.

"God, Help Me! I Can't Handle It!"

In that instant of desperation, panic hit me. Terrified, I blurted out in a yell, "God, help me! I can't handle it!"

I remembered that I had not even wanted to get drunk the night before. I'd played all the games alcoholics play—when I was out drinking I'd have just a beer an hour, or I'd drink only brandy—all the gimmicks to try to feel some kind of control. But I ended up just as drunk anyway.

I'll never forget my cry to God for help. And He answered. He took my drinking compulsion away completely. It was instantaneous. I knew it was not me; I did not do it. If you had asked me the day before if I believed in God, I would have told you that I didn't know, that I hadn't even really thought about it.

My crying out to God wasn't even a conscious prayer. It was like I had hit my thumb with a hammer—an instant reaction. Yet God heard and helped me. I realize it does not happen that way for everyone. But it did for me, and I am eternally grateful.

I made my desperate plea on a Wednesday morning. The following Friday night I went to an Alcoholics Anonymous (AA) meeting. Because of my father's involvement with AA when I was growing up (our entire family had been involved with AA activities), I was familiar with the program.

At the first meeting I was struck by the love and compassion flowing from the people in the room. These people had been to the bottom and had been humbled, but now had hope. On this particular night, most of those in attendance were older than I. One of them, a woman who appeared to have had a hard life, looked at me with great tenderness and said, "Honey, you are blessed. To find out your problem at a young age and to be here, you are blessed." Yes, I was, but I didn't yet know how much.

I read some of the AA materials, and the spiritual experience I'd had was reinforced in my thinking by AA's emphasis on a Supreme Being. After one of the meetings, someone mentioned to me that it seemed that only those who became Christians gained freedom from alcohol on a long-term basis. That caught my attention.

Religion still meant nothing to me, and I seldom went to church. But along about this time some dear friends, Tom and Linda Crocker, started telling me that the Bible was God's truth about life—His instructions on how to live given exactly as He intended them. This was too much for my skeptical mind to swallow.

"If you can show me how I can accept the Bible as the truth, logically with my brain, then I'll pay attention to what it has to say," I told Tom. "Otherwise, as far as I'm concerned, it's just another old book, a bunch of people's outdated philosophies or whatever, and I don't need it."

Yep, good old stubborn, show-me, prove-it-to-me, Norm! I thought I was throwing a big challenge at him, but Tom met me head-on and got me some books. Most notable were *More Than a Carpenter* and *Evidence That Demands a Verdict,* both by Josh McDowell.

These books carefully documented the validity of the claim that the Bible is indeed God's truth for mankind. I was overwhelmed by the objective evidence concerning the Bible from three major areas: archaeological discoveries, the history and weight of manuscript authenticity, and most of all, the proven fulfillment of Old Testament prophecy hundreds of years later in the New Testament.

I went over and over all the documented evidence presented so thoroughly in these books until I had no doubt left in my mind that the Bible is indeed the Word of God given to man—exactly as our friends the Crockers had claimed.

Stop the World and Let Me Off!

A couple of weeks prior to my dramatic cry to God for help, I had come home on Friday night after another week of travel, half loaded from drinking on the plane. Upon arriving at our house, I had poured myself another drink and walked out to the backyard. We were building a swimming pool and converting our garage into a cabana room. I stepped out there to check on what the workmen had completed that week, and I remember looking through the studs, drink in hand, and saying to myself, "Norm, you can also tear those doors off your bedroom and knock out that wall, and . . ." Then it dawned on me. Here I was already changing things, and yet I hadn't even finished and enjoyed *this* project. I asked myself in my alcohol fog, "Where's the payoff? Is this all there is to life? Then stop the world and let me off!"

"If you can show me how I can accept the Bible as the truth, logically with my brain, then I'll pay attention to what it has to say."

After becoming convinced of the truth of the Bible, I remembered that "Where's the payoff?" question. I had found an answer. I realized that there *is* more to life than chasing selfish dreams and desires. The *big* payoff comes from having a personal, faithful relationship with God Himself. Wow!

I no longer wanted the world to stop and let me off! I began to study the Bible and it dramatically changed my "control center" for living out my life.

Anne recalls that I would walk around the house with a Bible in my hands as I discovered the wonderful truths about Jesus. Life had taken on a new meaning. I wasn't trying so hard anymore to spit that hook out of my mouth.

5

CAUGHT BY THE MASTER FISHERMAN

I'm not a fence-sitter. I had read the Bible enough to know that it was decision time for me.

In the Bible it says that Jesus is "the way, the truth, and the life" (John 14:6). I'd been searching for the *way* that would bring me the *truth* resulting in *life*. I learned that we are slaves, not just to alcohol, bad habits, and other things, but overall to the big S word—*sin*. And sin is not acceptable to God.

I knew all this was true for me, and that I had sinned against God too. But the Bible also showed me that "the truth shall make you free" (John 8:32) and Christ is the Truth! I longed for freedom. I recognized that my choices and lifestyle had indeed separated me from God, and that I could never pay God for the wrongs of my life. I read and read and finally understood the fact that Jesus had died to pay for my sins, and that I needed to humble myself before God and trust Jesus alone for forgiveness and the ability to live life God's way. I understood that I could no longer avoid making a decision about Christ's claims.

So for two hours one night following a Bible study, I sat and talked with the leader, Myles Lorenzen, about some of my questions. Finally, at midnight, I accepted Christ through prayer, just as the Bible teaches. I accepted Jesus into my heart as my Lord and Savior. I saw that Jesus was God's only begotten Son and that through Him we have forgiveness of sins and the power for self-control to be free—finally and for real—from the physical and emotional control of sin.

When I got home after midnight, I went to our family room to be by myself. "Norm, what have you done?" I kept asking myself. But then I opened the Bible and asked God to confirm the commitment I'd made. I read the Bible, prayed, and then went to bed.

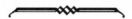

I'm not a fence-sitter. I had read the Bible enough to know that it was decision time for me.

The next morning I woke up convinced that I had done the right thing. From that moment on in 1974, I have never doubted my decision to put my faith in Christ for the remainder of my life.

My decision was made by my intellect through discerning the facts, and by my will in choosing to submit myself to God through accepting Christ's claims and His right to control my life. And now I've added to that all these years of personal experience, one-on-one with the living God. Words can't describe how wonderful life is in Christ!

I have a natural inclination to take things down to the basics. So it's no wonder that a Scripture of major importance to me has been Matthew 22 where Jesus was asked by a lawyer, "Which is the greatest commandment in the Law?" That's a question I might have asked Jesus if I had been in the lawyer's shoes.

Jesus' answer showed me how I could express my love for God and others: "'You shall love the Lord your God with all your heart, and with all your soul, and with all your mind.' This is the great and foremost commandment. The second is like it, 'You shall love your neighbor as yourself'" (vv. 37-39).

As I thought about Jesus' words, I had to ask myself if my thoughts and actions were pleasing to God. Was He happy with me? Were my goals and desires compatible with His reply to the lawyer? If not, I decided I'd better start praying about those areas in my life and work on getting them in line.

I told myself, "Norm, you need to want what He wants, and to love what He loves." To me this included *all* of me, and that meant my business life, too, which was so much a major part of what was going on in my life.

Jesus didn't add to that great commandment a clause that excluded one's business or vocation, or an exception that said "except while on vacation," or anything else. He let me know immediately it was for all of me, all of the time.

In all my initial inquiries and searching the Word of God, I decided that if I found something in any area of my life that didn't square with His way of doing things, I would have to make changes. So my approach was to go to God and His Word, to learn what He loves and wants, and to ask Him to help me love Him more.

Moreover, I asked Him to help me love—and want to love—others, and then to help me follow His leading in doing what He wants me to do, all the while confessing my sins and asking for His help. This keeps me in constant communion with Him since I can't, on my own, live a life that pleases Him.

No Longer Fighting the Hook

After I accepted Christ, at some point I remembered my Acapulco fishing trip and the experience of that big sailfish fighting the hook. Well, now the hook had been set . . . by God. The Master Fisherman had won. I no longer fought against His claim to my life.

Most of my earlier motivation to succeed in business had been the fear of failure. I drove myself so as not to fall behind my peers. Having now given my life to Christ, and having told Him He could make of me what He wanted, I was set free from fear of business failure. Sure, I still have to plan and work hard and seek excellence. But from that moment on I have striven to only want what Christ wants. He knows better than I do what is best for me, my family, and the business and resources that He has entrusted to me.

∿

When I stopped drinking after crying out to God, it was as if a lot of the causes for my drinking dried up as well. Whatever had been driving me—my insecurities probably being number one—God started working those things out and helping me to see that my value was in Christ, not things.

Anne's and my marriage became a lot better, too, but it didn't end all of our problems.

Anne has told me that after I became a Christian she thought, "Whew! Now we can live happily ever after." I did change drastically in some major areas of my life, such as my swearing, smoking, drinking, and partying. But I didn't exactly change overnight in some of my other old patterns of behavior.

There was a constant reevaluation of situations as they arose with our children, in particular our daughter, Tracey. And we were not always in agreement. One moment Anne would be accusing me of being too hard on Tracey, and the next day she would be hard on Tracey too.

After I became a Christian, I had to go back and do some repenting to my kids. I remembered an incident with Tracey some years before when she had come to me all excited and told me she had a new birthday because she had been "born again" because of accepting Jesus into her heart. I had just patted her on the head and said, "Oh, really, honey? That's nice," and kept reading the paper. When I made my own decision to follow Christ, I apologized to Tracey for being so insensitive.

If there's one thing I really would change if I could in raising my kids, I would have emphasized the positive more often. I was a great one for pointing out where they needed to improve, rather than building on what was already in great shape. You can rip a kid's self-image to shreds by always harping on what you think is wrong or not up to snuff.

A good friend of Anne's, Mary Fertitta, wisely counseled her that there is a gap in most of our lives that needs to be healed. Even as Christians, we must eventually go back and resolve some hurts, angers, and misunderstandings that may have shaped us since childhood.

After I became a Christian, I had to go back
and do some repenting to my kids.

I believe we all have these gaps, but most of us deny them until a crisis forces us to look deeper into the reasons why we do things. Until then, we can only mature so far in our Christian walk. This is one of the reasons why the Bible emphasizes the need for forgiveness— forgiving others, forgiving ourselves, and asking forgiveness of those we have hurt, whether intentional or not.

And Then There Were Two

After seeing the changes in me after my encounter with the Truth, Anne seemed to be seeking some answers herself. Together we went to a meeting where a man named Mal Couch was speaking. Afterward Anne went up to him with some of her questions about Christianity and the Bible. Mal said, "Wait a minute," and then he just opened up his Bible, turned some pages, and within a matter of minutes had answered three of her crucial questions.

On the way home that night, Anne turned to me and said, "This is just incredible!"

Shortly after that, one of Anne's friends, Bonnie Singleton, came to see her. Her husband, Major Jerry Singleton, was a POW in Vietnam for seven years. He was, in fact, still in Vietnam at the time. Anne excitedly told Bonnie about my becoming a Christian. Bonnie was so happy for me, but then she floored Anne by saying, "That's wonderful, Anne, now what about you?"

Anne responded, "What do you mean, 'what about me?' I'm already a Christian!"

On Bonnie's way out the door she gave Anne a little booklet. "I wish you'd take this," said Bonnie, "and read it when you get the chance."

Anne took the pamphlet, walked into our bedroom, and sat down on the bed to read it. At the end it had a prayer to pray if you wanted to accept Christ. Anne thought, *Well, I believe all this. Surely I've prayed this prayer at some time in my life. But what if I haven't? Does that mean I'm going to hell?*

So she prayed, "Lord, just count this as the time that I have accepted You if I've never done it before, and I want to receive Christ into my heart." She decided to quit worrying about all her questions and to trust God and believe what He said. At long last we were joined at the heart in the way God intended all along.

∿∿

After visiting a church or two, we eventually ended up attending a church that was meeting in the building of a company that had gone bankrupt. The builders had stopped construction because of the bankruptcy and were letting the church use the space for worship.

I remember the first time we attended. I noticed that the area where the chairs were set up for the meeting had studs but no Sheetrock. You could literally walk through what was supposed to be a wall into the sanctuary. *What kind of outfit is this?* I thought to myself.

We went in and sat down. There were maybe forty families there, and we worshiped with them that morning. As it was ending, I turned around and looked at Anne and said, "I don't know what to say, but this feels like the place we are supposed to be." I was comforted to find out that Anne was feeling the same way. And from that point on we and our children became "regulars" at Garland Bible Fellowship. It was an excellent church with two hours of straight Bible teaching on Sundays. We got involved and developed new friendships.

Sad to say, as we grew in our walk with the Lord and tried to become more obedient, some of our old friends drifted away. But God replaced them with many, many new ones.

Eventually Anne and I taught Sunday school, starting out teaching the two- and three-year-olds, and eventually the older kids. It was good training for both of us, as God led us through the formative years of our new life in Him.

We both were discipled primarily by the staff of wha is today Search Ministries (appendix 2) on a regular weekly basis. We invited our non-Christian friends to Bible studies and church, all the while learning more about our faith so that we could answer the same questions that we used to ask.

On our twenty-fifth anniversary Anne handwrote Psalm 112 and gave it to me as a means of expressing her gratitude to God.

During this time, Anne gave me a beautiful gift. She felt overwhelmed with thankfulness to God for what He was doing with our marriage and family. The awe of what was happening in our lives took her breath away, and she enjoyed watching me evolve from "hard-partying Norm" into a spiritual leader in the church and community.

On our twenty-fifth wedding anniversary Anne handwrote Psalm 112 and gave it to me as a means of expressing her gratitude to God.

Praise the LORD!
How blessed is the man who fears the LORD,
Who greatly delights in His commandments.
His descendants will be mighty on earth;

The generation of the upright will be blessed.
Wealth and riches are in his house,
And his righteousness endures forever.
Light arises in the darkness for the upright;
He is gracious and compassionate and righteous.
It is well with the man who is gracious and lends;
He will maintain his cause in judgment.
For he will never be shaken;
The righteous will be remembered forever.
He will not fear evil tidings;
His heart is steadfast, trusting in the LORD.
His heart is upheld, he will not fear,
Until he looks with satisfaction on his adversaries.
He has given freely to the poor;
His righteousness endures forever;
His horn will be exalted in honor.
The wicked will see it and be vexed;
He will gnash his teeth and melt away;
The desire of the wicked will perish.

~~~

I'm still praying and working on all this. Many times I fail miserably. It isn't magic. It is faith—a personal relationship with the God of all that is.

Entrusting God with my fears—including my pride and fear of what others would think or do as I sought to employ Christian principles and God's direction in the Interstate Battery business—was absolutely essential.

Hang on to your hat, the story isn't over yet!

PART TWO

The Life of Business

and

the Business of Life

CELEBRATING HARD WORK

6

The setting is the impressive, top-rated Loews Anatole Hotel in Dallas, Texas. The huge Chantilly Ballroom is crowded to capacity. A marching band strikes up a tune in the rear of the ballroom and comes marching down the aisles, baton-twirling cowgirls and all, headed for the stage.

The stage is set up like an old Wild West town complete with "The Green Top Mine," "Willie's Place," "The Interstate Hotel," the "Fire House" cactus, and howling coyote props and real horses. Real cowboys perform rope tricks while riding atop prancing horses, a show put on by World Championship rodeo riders, which includes a real rodeo clown. I don't know if the Chantilly Ballroom has ever seen anything like it before or will again. The whole scene is incredible, but it's just the beginning.

The stage is cleared and the spotlights turn to a cast of characters straight out of a Western movie. The crowd roars as Violet, Interstate Battery's prim and proper v-p of human resources, rides in on (are you ready for this?) the back of a two-ton bull, briefcase in hand.

My brother Tommy, president of Interstate, is attired in John Wayne cowboy duds with a black patch over one eye as he fingers a gun in the holster on his hip. Gene Wooldridge, executive vice president of sales, swaggers along as a Clint Eastwood look-alike, hand on the pistol on his hip, unshaven, lookin' mighty serious.

Len Ruby, executive vice president for marketing and distribution, dressed to the hilt in bandito chaps and a big sombrero, fingers his gun too.

Carlos Sepulveda, executive vice president of finance and administration, gambler-lookin' in a dressy, black Doc Holiday outfit, is tiltin' his hat bigtime. Like everyone else, he's wearing fancy boots with spurs.

Then a grubby lookin' character strolls along, strummin' a "geetar," looking mighty familiar with that red bandanna around his forehead and long graying ponytail hangin' down, dressed in faded blue jeans and a Farm Aid T-shirt. Is it Willie Nelson? Nope. It's me, earring and all!

All these dudes stroll up onto the stage and the crazy Willie-like guy on the end pokes his head around the lineup and gives out a big ol' Texas holler, "It's show time, folks!"

I believe in dreams, the kind that God plants
in our hearts as little seeds.

Who says business can't be fun? The 1994 Interstate Batteries convention with its cowpoke theme was just one of many such events we've hosted. The convention is eagerly anticipated and held every other year. We've also held conventions in Hawaii, Florida, California, and Tennessee at top-rated hotels and resorts.

Our independent distributors and their families come from across the United States, Canada, and Puerto Rico. They come for the update, the camaraderie, and the celebration. The 1994 "Branded for Success" convention brought 2,300 Interstate folks back to Dallas where the company got its start.

Later, at the "Taste of Texas" party, while I watched everyone having a good time celebrating our record of selling 9.6 million batteries for the past twelve months, my thoughts drifted back and I found myself reflecting on the beginning of it all.

The "Battery Man"

John Searcy, founder of Interstate Batteries, always said that he and I were "the perfect duo." He says that when he first met me as a young man he was impressed that I asked the right questions. I guess I've never stopped asking questions. I was thirsty to learn back then, and I'm still just as much of a sponge. And John was an excellent teacher and mentor.

In the U.S. in the early fifties, the "battery man" was often thought of as someone wearing acid-eaten clothes, driving an acid-leaking truck. Being a battery man himself, John knew this stereotype was pretty true and didn't like it. He set out to do things differently.

John had a nice-looking red Studebaker pickup truck, a high quality battery product to sell, and his clothes were neat and clean. John says, "I had decided that I didn't want to be just a 9 to 5 white-collar employee, working my life away in some giant corporation. I'd always dreamed of starting my own business and growing it into a national company. I never let go of that dream."

That's me to a T. I believe in dreams, the kind that God plants in our hearts as little seeds.

Late in 1952, John executed a contract with Gould National Battery's Dallas plant under the company name of Interstate Battery System (IBS). The name originated in John's mind as a result of President Eisenhower's push to get the interstate highway system built throughout the country.

John and his partner, Bill Keyes, then set up a series of distributorships. They treated them with respect and dedicated their efforts to making these distributors successful. When Keyes retired, John started to think about finding someone with whom he could entrust the company—someone who would have the same love for its principles, which included dedication to everyone involved in the company. Little did I know that God was moving me into the picture.

After selling the service station in Galveston, my father had gotten our family's Interstate distributor business started in the Memphis area. My sales route was in the surrounding counties and stretched for two hundred miles. One of the counties in my territory, Tunica County, Mississippi, was listed as the poorest county in the United States. I would drive my route truck down those long stretches of highway with cotton fields reaching to the horizon and few humans in sight, let alone any cities. It could get kind of lonely.

The "big boys" in the battery business back then were stores like Sears and Montgomery Ward. But around the same time that my dad and I were getting going with the Interstate distributorship, a national sales manager from one of the major manufacturers quit and also started his own midsouth battery business, headquartered in Memphis. It made for an interesting challenge as I began learning the battery business.

As you can probably tell by now, I like a challenge. I began to become more and more convinced that at least 80 to 90 percent of the people who sell batteries ought to have the kind my dad and I were selling. I was, and I still am, completely sold on the quality and value of our product and our service system.

I thought this new competitor was on some kind of an ego trip, because he put his own name on each of his batteries. So every time I saw a place where his batteries were sold, my competitive juices really flowed. I took it as a personal challenge to get our batteries into that place to replace his.

I remember spending many hours driving from town to town and route stop to route stop, trying to figure out ways I could outsell this fellow. One of the things I started doing was driving directly into the larger corporation-type plantations. I knew that they had a lot of equipment that needed good batteries. And it was a long way into the nearest town, so why not service them right where they were?

This approach worked, and I picked up many new accounts. I was young and aggressive. My competitor was aggressive, too, and that added fuel to my fire. It was an incentive to really "go for it" when I realized that we were starting to outsell him. It was like that children's game, King of the Mountain, where you see who can knock the other guy off the top of the hill. Plus, we needed the money as business expanded.

Interstate Battery System was growing nationally, as well. In 1964 John Searcy noticed that there were more people on my dad's business payroll than it could reasonably support. My brothers, Jimmy and Tommy, worked with us by that time too. John came to visit Memphis, and the next thing I knew he was offering me a job back at headquarters in Dallas.

I was, and I still am, completely sold on the quality and value of our product and our service system.

My first assignment from John proved to me once again why I admired him and his people-oriented way of doing business. We traveled to Pasadena, Texas, where the area's distributor had died suddenly, leaving his wife in a panic. She refused to allow any trucks to run or even open the warehouse. Left uncorrected, the situation would cost everyone money, lower the value of her business, and hurt the reputation of Interstate.

John convinced the distributor's son and the family's attorney that closing the business could leave the widow with nothing to sell. He presented an arrangement whereby we would send a field man to operate the business until it could be sold, guaranteeing that the widow would receive all the profits. Interstate would absorb the operation expenses until sold, and she would receive in cash the best possible price for the business.

John decided that I was the man for the job. It was a ticklish situation, one that even I, at age twenty-seven, knew was serious and had to be tackled with energy and integrity. Looking back, I am amazed at the amount of faith John had in me.

In the end, after the attorney persuaded the widow that it was more than a fair solution and that we had her best interests at heart, he said he'd never participated in a business transaction that was handled with such kindness. John tried to give me the credit, but it was his patience and willingness to consider the widow's best interests that earned Interstate its reputation as one of the fairest, most ethical companies around. He even set up a program, the Distributor Pension Fund, to allow for handling these same kinds of human problems that come up in business.

To recruit the caliber of distributors John wanted with his company, we began advertising in the business opportunity sections of newspapers and in a magazine called *The Gasoline Retailer*. One of his first ads read, "Working Man's Opportunity," and that's exactly what it was. From day one, John had the best interests of the working man at heart.

Our family had already experienced John's magnanimous heart. My father and John became good friends, and we benefited from his kindness and charitable nature. There wasn't a selfish bone in his body, no pride or self-seeking. He was a true gentleman's gentleman. A man of great humility.

So for me, the chance to work for John in his Dallas-based office was the opportunity of a lifetime.

Three Steps Forward, Two Steps Back

After moving from Memphis to Dallas, I hit the road for Interstate in January of 1965. Immediately I began traveling the entire continental United States, selling distributorships and then setting them up and training them in the system. All the while I was learning the marketing trade.

One week it would be distributors, then the next week I'd be right out there on the street going from dealer to dealer, trying to set them up to retail our batteries. Sometimes at night I would do distributorship work on the telephone or work on graphic design for labels, brochures, and cartons. I had varying responsibilities, and I wore these different hats for many years. This meant being away from home a lot. I once added up all the states where I had sold batteries dealer-to-dealer down the street, and the total was forty-three states.

Sometimes we encountered obstacles and problems that had to be solved, and I'd tell Anne, "It's like taking three steps forward and two steps back." But I was developing a marketing sense that would prove to be invaluable in the years ahead. It was truly a "working man's opportunity" for me too. I was sold on the concept and worked at presenting it that way to prospective distributors and dealers wherever I went.

In terms of my personality, the work fitted me perfectly. I remember taking a personality profile test one time that rated needs—high or low—in facets of our personality. A score of one hundred would indicate great need; a zero would be no need. The result was a U-shaped curve. In the degree of need for *change,* I was around a ninety-six. This indicated that I thrived on change.

So the thing that was good about the Interstate Battery job was that I worked on many different things, and I would go from area to area. And even though the selling and training were always the same, it was in a different place with different people and different circumstances, and that met a big need in my life. One week I might be in San Diego, California, and the next in Wichita Falls, Texas. I was constantly chipping away at this big ol' U.S.A., but it seemed like a new game each week.

When I was selling directly on the street to service stations, garages, car dealers, and places like that, it was all cold selling, just loading up the batteries in the trunk of my rental car (later we switched to station wagons and eventually vans) and taking off from the warehouse. In every instance I was trying to get these places to take the batteries on consignment. My attitude going in was always optimistic—who could resist something that was good quality, with better service, priced right, and would be left on consignment? It's surprising how many did!

The Rewards of Trust and Wisdom

Recently one of our men in the Dallas office said to me, "It's sure easy to work for somebody when you trust them 100 percent." He likened it to a really great marriage relationship, and I knew just what he was saying.

John Searcy made it easy for me to trust him, and I have sought to follow in his footsteps with everyone who becomes a part of our Interstate team. Just like I learned in my relationship with Joe Gibbs years later, trust is a key element in any relationship.

It came into my mind one day that if you are working for somebody and you waste your time, it is no different from putting your hand in the cash register.

I might be considered hard-drawn on this matter of trust and the importance of putting in an honest day's work for honest dollars. This work ethic is one of the principles that my own father ingrained in me. It wasn't a matter so much of honesty or dishonesty; it was just that this was the right thing to do.

I don't remember ever thinking about stealing anything from anybody on any job I ever had. It came into my mind one day that if you are working for somebody and you waste your time, it is no different from putting your hand in the cash register. If I was supposed to be working, and I told somebody that I was going to be in Minnesota doing sales calls, busting my tail to sell batteries, and then I dillydallied around at all, I really felt guilty. I didn't like that feeling and avoided it by doing the job at hand in the best possible way.

And in this area, John Searcy was a wonderful role model. He was an honest, hardworking guy who was smart, but he was also compassionate and considerate. I remember him saying, "When I lay my head down at night, I want to be able to feel good about what I've done so I can go to sleep."

I decided that was a great philosophy, and I was going to work at it.

I also remember John carrying in his wallet a quote from the Bible. It was the Proverbs 3:1-7 passage. Every morning he would take that scrap of paper out and read it. That was his prayer and inspirational thought for the day. It really made an impression on me. The words go like this:

> *My son, do not forget my teaching,*
> *But let your heart keep my commandments;*
> *For length of days and years of life,*
> *And peace they will add to you.*
> *Do not let kindness and truth leave you;*
> *Bind them around your neck,*
> *Write them on the tablet of your heart.*
> *So you will find favor and good repute*
> *In the sight of God and man.*
> *Trust in the LORD with all your heart,*
> *And do not lean on your own understanding.*
> *In all your ways acknowledge Him,*
> *And He will make your paths straight.*
> *Do not be wise in your own eyes;*
> *Fear the LORD and turn away from evil.*

The Embryo: Ten Years of Learning the Business

As I pitched Interstate, I would tell prospective distributors that this wasn't a "get in and get rich quick" deal. It was a business opportunity that, for the right person, would be a rewarding business, both in terms of providing a good, secure living and also a rightful pride in what they were doing. We always assured distributors we would protect the areas assigned to them and, in fact, we have always bent over backward to do that very thing.

Early on when we went full-scale national, there were "virgin" territories to open up all over. A man could get into the business instantly with very little capital outlay and often after the first ninety days he'd be making enough profit to cover his living expenses. This was a good deal for Interstate, too, because we just kept piling volume on top of volume by opening more and more new distributorships as we worked at covering all of the U.S.

The success of the batteries themselves (credit for living up to the claims we made for them goes to our manufacturer—Globe Union then and Johnson Controls now) spurred the growth of the business to where we are today, with over ten million batteries sold per year.

We encountered some square pegs trying to fit into round holes, and the challenge to encourage and help develop individual distributors and their dealer base was a big one. We stuck our necks out at times, and I had to make value judgments that weren't always easy. But I always came back to the basic principle that John had instilled in me: Put the distributor first, protect his interests and investment, take care of our employees, treating them fair and square, and then this will be reflected to the customer who will also be happy and satisfied. A simple "Do unto others as unto yourself" business philosophy, but a sound one that God Himself has given us!

As we began to grow and become more and more successful, we had to start monitoring territories and holding people accountable for their agreed market penetration in those territories. When they weren't producing, we had to either help them come to terms with why they weren't growing and get it going, or work out a territory split so that we could give somebody else the opportunity. And we're still in that kind of operative mode.

There were times at the outset when I'd have to go to John and say, "Hey, John, I think I screwed up. I might have messed up that deal *big time.*"

John was great. After a slap on the back and some kind words—"I like you being up front about it, Norm,"—we'd begin to try and make the best out of the situation.

Sometimes I'd slack up some, but having developed into a conscientious and hard worker, I'd work at ways to make it up to the company. I found a sense of humor helped too.

Most of the fellows who traveled and trained with me in earlier days are still with us today—ten, fifteen, even twenty years later. Usually a man would start out in the warehouse for a period of time, then we'd move him up to what we called the "hotshot man" (taking care of call-in deliveries), and lastly he'd train as a local route manager before hitting the road—usually as a national sales rep. He could go on from there as his performance and our growth dictated.

There were times at the outset when I'd have to go to John and say, "Hey, John, I think I screwed up."

In our travels I sought to instill into these men the importance of treating people with respect, telling them things like: "These people you deal with are the lifeblood of our business, and it's wise to listen to them and consider their opinions. They are our customers, they have as much sense as we do, and deserve kind, respectful treatment."

Resilience and Flexibility

I had to learn many basic principles myself, so I was a learner right along with the guys I was training. I quickly found out how important it was to be resilient and flexible. My basic nature is to be a scrapper, a fighter of sorts, and I had to learn to rein that in and put it to use productively. When something went wrong, I had to seek solutions and impart them to those who might have been a part of the problem. It caused me to start honing in on "reading" people and situations, trying to understand where the person was coming from. I had to learn patience, too, in dealing with people. This wasn't a quality that came easily to me, but knowing that most people want "win-win" situations, and since I was to be a people-manager, I concentrated on being alert for creative solutions.

"Go in well prepared, have your background research firmly fixed in your mind," I urged the men, and I worked on practicing it myself. "Treat this like it's your own business," I'd add. I treated the company credit card like it was my own money. "Sacrifice a little now and then," I told the guys. "It will not only make you feel good about yourself, but it usually comes back to you several fold to boot." I've never asked anybody to do something for the company that I haven't done or wouldn't do myself.

The men saw me get angry on occasion, but I tried to control that and apologized later when I knew I had been out of line.

I once told Mike Wier, one of our vice presidents who has been with us a long time, "Just remember that I make some management calls that you may not agree with, or may not like, but I ask that you always trust me, and if you don't understand it, tell me. If we're in a building and I'm on the tenth floor and you're on the third floor and we're each looking out the window, who can see farther?" Mike got the point.

A Fair Shot

When my brother Tommy joined us in 1969, we were selling about a half million batteries a year. He fit right in and was a tremendous help in developing the U.S. market, setting up dealers and building up our distributors. We were still setting up all these distributorships in virgin territory, so it was all incremental growth to us. Each year as the distributors and dealers matured and sold more, we would be adding more accounts.

I knew that as long as we had x-number of men on the street, making x-number of sales calls, getting x-number of new dealers who, in turn, would sell more batteries, it was indeed a numbers machine at that point. Not that we treated the people as numbers—far from it!—but we were in an upward-spiraling growth mode. The demand for the product was there, and our own networking system was working. Even at that point, I basically had a twenty-year vision. Obviously, it's so important to have a well-defined goal. Then all you have to do each day is just go out and chip away at it and not worry about things. But you do have to stick with it, and sometimes it takes a long time to arrive at the destination.

"Give everybody a fair shot," I told Tommy and the guys. "That's all anybody expects." Some of the men we hired really took that ball and ran with it. Some didn't.

Most of those who did are still with Interstate today, holding down positions or distributorships they've earned because of talent, hard work, and the ability to grow with the new demands and the changing times.

Leading by Example

John Searcy, like any good mentor, led by example. He had an open-door policy; you knew you could always go to him with a problem or an idea. I've sought to follow his leading. The principles by which he led empowered everyone to act without constant monitoring, correcting, evaluating, or controlling. But we were also held accountable. The payoff resulted in more creativity and expertise and a good feeling of shared responsibility at all levels of the organization.

Go the Extra Mile

John Searcy was always willing to go the extra mile with somebody. Because of this and other qualities, he had a great reputation. Fortunately, when it came my turn to lead Interstate, I was able to pigtail on his reputation.

The challenge, of course, was not only to maintain what John so magnificently had begun, but to enlarge and expand it, which was what he wanted, deserved, and expected. God enabled us to do so.

The critics are always going to be around. John warned me about that. "Don't think you won't encounter them," he cautioned, "because any time you are dealing with people and their work and money, they won't always agree with you. You will have to make tough decisions."

John encouraged me, however, by reinforcing something he'd said earlier when he complimented me on being a good thinker and a decisive person. "I know I can trust you to make good decisions," he said. This gave me confidence and inspired me to try even harder.

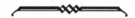

"Give everybody a fair shot," I told Tommy and the guys. "That's all anybody expects."

John Searcy had all the attributes of a great businessman. He was (and still is) a hard worker. He was smart and wise—a systematic thinker. I really admired that quality in him as I saw him think things through and then act on those thoughts. He was very positive—he had this "Go for it" attitude. He wasn't overly cautious, but somewhat calculating—a necessary quality in a successful businessman.

John is just a truly good guy, and the whole basis for the success of our business lies with John Searcy and the system he founded.

STRATEGIC MOVES

7

J ohn Searcy had a philosophy that rubbed off on me. "Life's too short," he'd say as we discussed company growth potential. We elected to grow as we desired. I'm sure Interstate Batteries could have grown a lot faster—whether our decision was wrong or right is moot—but we agreed that just because the opportunities were there, we weren't going to forget that life's too short to be pushing ourselves into one high-risk move after another.

We concluded that if any decision wasn't reasonably comfortable and within a reasonable work ethic and a sound financial risk/reward approach, we just weren't going to do it. And of course, uppermost at all times was the well-being of our distributors, their employees, the Interstate Batteries dealers, and our corporate employees.

WATERSHED TIMES

Growth at Interstate over the years has always been reasonably steady, but there have been some watershed events when very significant things happened.

One of these occurred early on for me when John Searcy was still president and chairman of the board. It happened in 1966 at the time when Congress elected to remove the 8 percent excise tax from batteries (and a lot of other items). The excise tax had been paid to the government by the manufacturer, who passed the cost on to Interstate as part of the cost of our batteries.

When Globe Union, our manufacturer, no longer had to pay this tax, they lowered our cost, and we, in turn, were able to pass the lower price right on through to our distributors.

It became clear to Searcy that those distributors who owed Interstate Batteries "special" money, which we had advanced them for inventory expansion, could pay their debts simply by our continuing to invoice them at the old excise-taxed price and then, at the end of the month, applying the appropriate credit to their debt. It was actually an overbill.

Taking risks, though, is what Interstate Battery System was built on from the beginning.

In order to help distributors grow, Interstate had financed a lot of them with extended credit, but we were getting pretty strung out. Many distributors owed us quite a bit of money, beyond what was really considered normal terms. So we retained the monies from the excise tax refund/reduction to allow these distributors to pay down their accounts automatically on a per battery basis.

When the debt was fully paid, the overbill was dropped and the distributor was invoiced at the regular current price. It really helped by enabling them to build equity in their business. It helped us to gain leverage on the competition and, over a period of time, it allowed us to become much stronger financially. It was definitely a win-win situation for everyone.

On another occasion, back when we had a front label on our batteries, we came up with a molded design for the top of the batteries.

"Hey, once the battery is in the car, people don't see the side of it much anyway," I said to John one day. "So if we can make the top attractive, we can drop the front label and save ten cents a battery."

That ten cents was a big plus since we were having some financial struggles at the time. The added bonus was that the top design was very attractive and actually enhanced the battery appearance. So it was a double win. We were able to give the distributor what we considered a better looking battery and still save ten cents a unit, which helped us to fund more expansion and the things that needed to be done to encourage growth and stabilize the company.

Nationwide Refunding: The Operator 25 Program

In order to assure nationwide warranty service to all Interstate Battery purchasers and our dealers, in 1965 Searcy took a chance on a relatively new program: Western Union's Operator 25 program. The program was designed to give purchasers of any product a nationwide phone number to call if that product needed servicing anywhere in the United States. The same number could be used should a customer wish to buy that product.

Searcy envisioned this as an especially valuable benefit for the customer who experienced battery problems in more isolated areas, far from an Interstate dealer. If this happened, the Western Union operator would advise the customer to buy a battery of his choice and mail the Interstate date ring and label to the Interstate home office. From there we would mail directly to the customer a refund for the unused portion of the warranty.

John Searcy was way ahead of the pack. Our competitors, and even our suppliers, thought this nationwide refunding of unused warranty was a very risky business. Taking risks, though, is what Interstate Battery System was built on from the beginning—that and innovations that clearly separated the system from all other battery sellers in the United States.

We closely monitored the cost of these refunds with the Operator 25 program, and it turned out to be amazingly low, averaging only the cost of one new battery for every four thousand batteries sold.

Even though others worried about this program, John really never did sweat it. After all, he was convinced that it was the right thing to do and that he had the best batteries on the market. He proved himself right!

In addition, an unexpected benefit came when the first batteries with the Western Union labels were used in soliciting new dealers. In new territories where dealers had never heard of Interstate batteries, they all knew and respected Western Union. That fact alone gave Interstate Battery some clout it never had before, making retailer prospects much more receptive to our dealership program.

1-800-CRANK-IT Hotline

As the United States (and now Canada) gradually filled with Interstate dealers, the purpose of the Western Union number shifted toward providing locations of dealers nearest any customer needing an adjustment or a new battery. A toll-free nationwide warranty phone number has been on every Interstate battery sold for at least twenty-five years.

In more recent years the demand for our batteries has grown so much that we've added a toll-free number exclusively for the location of dealers (by zip code) who sell our batteries by specific use, such as automotive, marine, commercial, or motorcycle. That number is 1-800-CRANK-IT. I love it!

Unit Profit

I don't know how many times I've proved to myself that you just never go wrong in treating the other person fair and square. Take our battery exchange program, for example.

There was a time when the price of lead jumped way up, and because the cost of batteries is based on the value of lead, the price of batteries climbed way up too. However, Interstate has always sold batteries on an exchange basis; when a dealer sells a new battery, he gives us an old battery back in exchange.

So when the price of lead goes up and we have to pay more for new batteries, we automatically get paid more for the old batteries. This keeps our pricing on both the wholesale and retail level stabilized.

In the early days, most of our competitors didn't have this sell/exchange program, so they weren't able to offset the price increases when lead skyrocketed. They were operating on a percentage of profit basis, which is normal—all accounting principles operate on percentages. But at that time, we weren't. We operated on unit profit and kept things very simple. If one of our distributors made six dollars on a battery and sold six thousand batteries, he would make $36,000 gross profit. If it took $12,000 to run the business, he had earned $24,000.

I don't know how many times I've proved to myself that you just never go wrong in treating the other person fair and square.

By selling on an exchange basis and not operating on percentages, we weren't continually adjusting our prices as new battery costs kept going up, solely because of lead price increases. The end result was that prices got out of line in the battery business, but Interstate was substantially under the competition—always a nice place to be if you can do it and make a profit. This really helped us get established with new car dealerships across the country. We were able to go in, sell low, and build relationships based on trustworthiness, quality, service, and everything the automotive world expects and desires in a supplier. We won many of them to our way of doing business.

Since our batteries were always priced fairly, we didn't have to get into any price wars. This gave us a big foothold in the market with continued advantage for more growth.

Gas Shortages at the Pump

Watershed opportunities? Yes, most successful businesses have them and can point to such events that gave them a boost in their particular market.

Well, are you old enough to remember the great gasoline shortages of the seventies? It's kind of hard to believe now, but service stations could hardly get enough gas to stay open a few hours a day. This really scared us at Interstate because most of our business was in service stations. We had some garages and other places where dealers sold our batteries, but the bulk of the business was still with the corner service stations.

While our field men and salesmen were still going out all over the country trying to open new dealers to boost our distributors, we began to see those mile-long gas lines. Many service stations had to close several hours per day. They just couldn't get gas.

Our field men and salesmen that were trying to make calls couldn't even get near the station owner to talk to him about placing our batteries on consignment. The poor guy was up to his neck in alligators just trying to get gas and stay in business. Moreover, rumor had it that gas was going up to three dollars a gallon. It was a major time of uncertainty.

We told our fellows to not back off and "hang tight." Almost everyone in the business, if they were at all aggressive, quit being so and went into limbo. Back at our corporate headquarters in Dallas we looked at each other dumbfounded. Still, we figured there had to be a way out of this. After all, people still needed batteries.

I was one of the field men out there trying to think of ways to solve this dilemma. "We can't just operate on emotion and the general negative consensus in people's minds," I told myself. Finally, John Searcy and I settled on a simple strategy and got the word out to all our field men that we were going to just keep going and keep trying. Our instructions weren't exactly profound, but it worked: "Just sell 'em. Find marine shops, tire stores, fleets, lawn and garden centers, tractor dealers, farm co-ops, garages, car dealerships, recreational vehicles—go anywhere you can sell them that's not related to gasoline."

When calling mostly on service stations, Interstate used to average setting up twenty new accounts a week per man. So the challenge was to see if we could keep our average up without finding as many service stations. Amazingly, we did! And we practically had the playing field to ourselves. It was like a lot of the other players went home and were just wondering, waiting, and watching. We hammered like crazy out there.

The second benefit from this strategy was it diversified our account base. Where we were mentally geared in one direction with, for example, 200,000 service stations, because of the adversity we faced, the playing field suddenly opened up a 300,000 account potential. Now we had a bigger target.

It was a matter of taking a tough situation and turning it into something good as we introduced our batteries into all these different businesses. It was a plus for them; it was diversification for us, enabling us to really penetrate a whole new market.

At the outset of Interstate Batteries' history, there were upward of 220,000 service stations doing automotive repairs, as well as service. Today, there are less than 80,000. A big transition has taken place with 140,000 service stations gone. Many were replaced with auto repair garages, tire stores, and the like. So the source and locations of places for batteries have changed radically over the years.

"Y'all Haulin' Minnows?"

We laugh about it now, but it wasn't so funny years ago, before we had our big green and white Interstate Batteries trucks traveling the highways nationwide. Way back then, our trucks weren't identified. We didn't advertise on them.

This was deliberate. The theory was that without identification we could go into the big, nice service stations that were branded, such as Exxon, Texaco, and Shell. They had their own brand of batteries, of course, but we could slide in there and provide them better batteries with better service and at a better price.

The oil company bosses wanted only *their* brands in *their* stations. So, many times our batteries were hidden in the back rooms so the station owners wouldn't be pressured or hassled by the oil company reps. For all anyone knew, our trucks looked like we were pulling in there buying junks, or as they used to say to us in southern

Mississippi, "Y'all haulin' minnows?" And to be honest, they kind of looked like minnow trucks used then in the South.

By 1980 we'd covered the nation pretty well, so we began to identify our trucks and use them for graphic promotion. Today we have over a thousand rolling signs (our trucks) dedicated to serving over 200,000 Interstate dealers all across the U.S. and Canada.

Advertising and Promotion

I had taken commercial art in college and liked it. Early on in my Interstate days, I was involved in designing the cartons, brochures, slip sheets, price sheets, window signs, and other types of promotional materials.

I'd sketch this stuff on airplanes, at night in hotel rooms, and, of course, at the Dallas office. I enjoyed drawing, and it afforded some variety, which matched well with my emotional makeup.

The oil company bosses wanted only their brands in their stations. So, many times our batteries were hidden in the back rooms so the station owners wouldn't be pressured or hassled by the oil company reps.

Today Interstate has a very large marketing division, with dozens of men and women in the areas of marketing, advertising, public relations, and statistics. They are wonderful individuals who make up a great team and do a great job. But I still doodle ideas on napkins now and then.

A Numbers Game, Not a Glamorous Kind of Deal

In 1976 we had our first one million batteries sales year. We doubled that by 1978 when John Searcy retired. Then in 1980 we broke the three million mark, and in 1982, four million. In September of 1995 we hit ten million battery sales on a running twelve-month basis, and the following month we sold over one million units; both of these figures broke U.S. records for a company like ours! (No sales and distribution company had ever sold over 9.2 million in twelve months.)

Through all of these busy years, my wife, Anne, was the mortar that held our marriage together. Her stability and long-suffering strike me now more than ever as being the kind of stuff every man wishes his wife were made of—she *was* and *is* very special. One of her best qualities is just being a good listener.

Sometimes I'd come home and grumble to her. "You know some of my friends are into some really glamorous kinds of jobs," I'd say. "They aren't out driving battery trucks and picking up filthy junk batteries and going around in a uniform. They're wearing a coat and tie and driving some of those fancy company cars."

Anne would look at me with her beautiful blue eyes, a soft expression on her face, head tilted, as I continued. "Yeah, some of those guys are selling women's clothes to Neiman Marcus, or they're stock-brokers or bankers. And when they ask me, 'Hey Norm, what are you doing these days?' and I mention Interstate Batteries, nobody knows what I'm talking about. Nobody knows about the battery business, Anne," I'd complain. "So I tell them I sell batteries to service stations and garages, and it's kind of like they respond with 'Ho-hum . . .'"

From an ego standpoint, it wasn't a glamorous kind of a deal. But I was very fortunate and deep down inside I knew it. I remember someone asking me what I was doing, and I responded that I didn't care if I had to carry junk batteries through the lobby of the Fountain-bleau Hotel in Miami Beach, as long as I was being paid enough.

But every so often, when I'd get down in the mouth, I had to ask myself some questions and that would help light a spark of more positive thoughts. "One, are you making a fair wage for what you are doing? Two, are you learning something—are you learning so that no matter what happens, you will be better equipped and wiser than when you started? And three, does it look like there is a future at Interstate?" The answer, of course, was yes to all three questions.

I would tell myself to shut up and quit worrying about the other stuff. Of course, I couldn't even begin to imagine what that future might be, but I had a wife and two kids to support and I liked the challenge. That helped keep me on course.

Attitude: The Mind's Paintbrush

How grateful I am today that my attitude problem was short-lived. I got it out of my system and that was that. I understand that Mary Crowley, a remarkable Dallas entrepreneur, had a wonderful philosophy relative to one's attitude that she passed on to all her Home Interiors and Gifts managers. Mary said, "You never gain by sitting around feeling sorry for yourself. Attitude is the mind's paintbrush. It can color a situation gloomy and gray, or cheerful and bright. In fact, attitudes are more important than facts." I like that.

Chuck Swindoll, one of the greatest thinkers in the country today, a theologian, author, and now president of Dallas Theological Seminary, has a chapter entitled "Go For It!" in his book *The Quest for Character.* In that chapter he talks about how few people there are who see beyond the danger, who say to those on the edge of some venture, *"Go for it!"*

The problem, Swindoll says, is not a lack of potential, it's a lack of perseverance. How much more could be accomplished if only there were more brave souls urging others on, affirming them, regardless of the risks.[1]

At Interstate our philosophy has always been to go for it, even when circumstances strongly suggest the opposite. Life *can* and *should* be a great adventure. Our work *can* and *should* be fun. Sure there are boulders to get around, hurdles to jump over, but we *can be* trailblazers.

As leaders we are expected to be stable and strong, mature and full of wisdom and discernment. I know this and certainly have respect for those I've had the good fortune to know who exemplify these qualities, in particular John Searcy. But knowing myself, I recognize that I have a long way to go.

Mediocrity Versus Excellence

As I've thought about mediocrity versus excellence, I am reminded of how I developed my philosophy about this and how I sought to transmit this in a motivational sort of way to our people at Interstate, especially in the earlier days when I was seeking good men with long-term potential.

I remember thinking, *Well, everyone has to work.* Very few people have the financial means to not have to work to earn a living and make their way through life. So you begin with the fact that there are a certain number of givens in life that we are required to do. Work is one of them.

You begin with the basics—getting up in the morning and making yourself presentable so you are "workable." Then, once at work, you have to do sufficient activities to maintain your job. So when I added all that up, I could see that those are the "fixed costs," as it were, and that everyone has a basic fixed cost that they have to pay in order to earn a living.

At Interstate our philosophy has always been
to "go for it," even when circumstances
strongly suggest the opposite.

The issue then becomes: What percentage of performance do you think people have to make in order to keep their jobs? So when I'd talk to our men, I'd ask them, "What do you want out of life?" The answer was uniformly similar—everyone wants success, happiness, and some fun in life too. They also want to do a good job.

Then I asked them: "If we figured that 100 percent is excellent, what percentage do you think you have to do to keep a good job?" Most everyone responded with between 70 and 85 percent. So let's say that 75 percent is what you have to perform in order to just keep your job. The issue then becomes: What's excellent?

Excellence, let's say, is 90 percent, give or take a few percentage points. So the difference between being excellent or mediocre—just getting by in a job—can be as little as 15 percent. So if you add that to your daily goals, achieving excellence means you only need to crank up your efforts, crank up your thinking, crank up paying attention to what you are doing, crank up your commitment, and if you want to, crank up your time by that 15 percentage points.

What is 15 percent of a forty-hour workweek? It's only six hours. An hour and fifteen minutes a day can mean coming in twenty minutes early, leaving twenty minutes late, and only taking a half hour for lunch. And in my book that can be the difference between excellence and mediocrity. Not too big a price to pay!

On top of that, I asked myself: "Who do you think enjoys their job?" Well, it's usually those who are bragged on who do well and are excellent, because excellence gets recognition. So, you see where I'm going with this? One, people want recognition; through excellence they can get recognition. Two, who usually gets the advancements and the higher-paying positions? It's usually the excellent people—the hardworking, committed people who are making things happen. And then, three, who usually gets the better jobs, the fun stuff, the challenges where they can get things going and make things happen? It's those who are in the forefront, those who are really excellent.

So those things that everybody wants—that you want and I want—really are only 15 percent beyond where we may already be.

Excellence is attainable. From a simplistic standpoint, the issue is to figure out how you're going to get to it from where you are now. For example, the one area alone of coming in early and staying late doesn't have to be a family killer.

I would not have understood this kind of thinking on excellence at one time in my life. But today, after hammering out my personal philosophy of the rewards of work and the difference between mediocrity and excellence, I'm eager to share what I've learned. In a nutshell, my advice to anyone aspiring to move beyond mediocrity and the status quo, is to crank it up—whatever it takes—and go for it!

A SOVEREIGN PLACEMENT

8

S ome would say what happened to me in taking over the reins of Interstate Batteries was luck. I would say it was a sovereign placement by God. Moreover, others who were a part of Interstate at that time and who stayed with the company, and still others who shortly thereafter became an integral part of the management team, have all been, I believe, truly godsends.

The original agreement that John Searcy orchestrated was for him to retire at age sixty-six, which would have been in 1982. Instead, John chose to leave at sixty-two. It was a surprise, but John had arranged things so well that I was able to move into the position of president and chairman of the board with ease.

No Shortcut to Experience

In John's words, there's no shortcut to experience. I had been in the battery business since 1962 and had worked for him since 1965. My brother Tommy, who eventually took my place as president, came on board in November 1969; and in 1971, Gene Wooldridge, who later became our executive vice president of sales and marketing, joined forces with Interstate. Each of us had our special niche in the company, and our personalities were such that we complemented one another. We had plenty of mutual respect and trust.

I am more of a creator and a do-it-yourself type, while my

brother Tommy, is an implementer. In other words, he likes to make things work and run harmoniously and likes getting things done through others.

Tommy had been in charge of distribution and working with distributors, seeing to it that things flowed from that direction. I had been vice president of marketing and sales, and John Searcy kept the financial side of the business on a sure footing. After John's retirement, Tommy took over as chief financial officer until 1980.

The relationship Tommy, Gene, and I shared was a strong working bond and it was greatly cemented by our common faith in Christ. This is not to say we didn't have personality differences, because we did and do. But we were able to respect each other's differences and work together twenty-four years to build Interstate into a strong, successful battery company.

"I stood back and thought, Man, this guy is meticulous. This is unbelievable. It would have taken me all of thirty seconds to buy socks!"

Another key player at Interstate Batteries is Len Ruby, who was an employee of Johnson Controls until February 1979. We needed someone who understood the technical/manufacturing side of the business, and Len's experience at Johnson Controls uniquely qualified him for what we needed. Today Len serves as executive vice president of marketing and distribution.

Len recalls how his hiring took place: "We talked a little about salary and benefits. I'd been working for a big company, and I pulled out this fancy notebook describing all the benefits. Norm had asked David Brinson, Interstate's comptroller, to pull together the company's package. Norm opened up his desk drawer and pulled out a loose-leaf, half sheet of paper with holes in it. This was the benefit package!

"Then we started talking about the job and the benefits. The net result was that Interstate had a better package on its half sheet of paper than I had in the fancy package! Their profit sharing plan was excellent. Everything about the company appealed to me.

"Just about everybody with their wives, and my wife, Peggy, and I, went out to dinner that night, and what it said to me was 'Here's a real family.' Norm, being the excellent salesman that he is, sold me. Before the evening was over, he looked at me and the other ten couples and said, 'You know, you're really going to have to take this job because I don't know if I can afford to interview any other guys!'"

Len brought to Interstate an asset that we hadn't quite counted on—his sense of humor and the fun kind of fellow that he is. Len won't let me forget a trip the two of us made to southern California to visit the Johnson Controls plant in Fullerton. We had some extra time, and I said to him, "I need to buy some socks. Let's find a mall."

It was 1979 and Len was new to the company; he didn't know me too well. He was pretty young and still sort of feeling his way around. He had no clue about my shopping habits. I was looking for a certain kind of men's socks that I really like. Finally, after about the fourth store, I found what I wanted. "Hey, man," I said, "these are the socks!" and I shelled out the money. Len tells the rest of the story like this:

"I stood back and thought, *Man, this guy is meticulous. This is unbelievable. It would have taken me all of thirty seconds to buy socks!*"

The real capper, however, according to Len, is that three years later I called him one day.

"Ruby!" I said.

"Yeah, Norm, what do you want?"

"You know a couple of years back when we were in southern California?"

"Sure. Why?"

"Remember we went to that store and bought socks?"

"Yeah, Norm. For sure, you bought socks!"

"Do you know what the brand was?"

"No, Norm, I don't know what the brand was."

"Hmm, I was hoping you'd remember. I've got to find those same socks again!"

My wife doesn't find this too unusual. She says I am a very tactile person, that I like for things to "feel right," even my socks! She likes to tell about my quirky habit of pulling my socks down at night when I'm relaxing, so that they are half on and half off my feet. My explanation is simple and, for me, logical: All the way off, my feet get cold; all the way on, they are hot; halfway on, they are just perfect! She calls this a "Normism." The funny thing is, our son, Scott, does the same thing!

Len says that's the way I am about everything. He also likes to tell about how we got lost trying to find our way back to the Los Angeles airport. He says we were on one of the freeways and we knew we were going west, the right direction, but we hadn't a clue where the airport actually was. Len claims that I said, "Stick your head out the window, Ruby, and see if you can spot any planes." He insists that while I was driving, I had him hanging out the window, checking out the sky.

We have had our share of fun and laughs at Interstate—all of us. I'm convinced God has a great sense of humor, so at Interstate we try to enjoy what we're doing and have some fun. Everything just goes better when you have a smile on your face.

As a side note (remember, I *like* to take rabbit trails!), my definitions of happiness and joy are:

- Happiness comes from the outside and kind of settles on your mind and heart for a while and then it's gone. It's an "outside to the inside, over and over" kind of thing.
- Joy comes from having Christ in your heart. It begins on the inside and grows and flows to the outside forever. It's an "inside to the outside once and for always" kind of thing!

Ethics and Business Principles

Len Ruby recalls another incident that happened after he first came on board with us. As he tells it, I said to him: "Len, there's a competitor that I want you to check out. I think they are directly drop shipping batteries, and I don't agree with their procedure. I want you to find out about it."

"Okay, Norm, I think I know who this guy is."

He came back about twenty minutes later and said, "Here's the guy's whole program."

"How did you get that?" I responded.

"I called the guy," Len said.

"Did he tell you his whole program, knowing who you were and where you are now working?" I asked him.

"No," Len stated. "I just called him and said I owned ten service stations in Des Moines."

I'm convinced God has a great sense of humor,

so at Interstate we try to enjoy what we're

doing and have some fun.

"And that's how you got all this information?" I questioned him.
"Yeah."

"You lied to the guy," I said. "I don't ever want to put you or anyone else in that position. That's not what I intended for you to do in order to find out what was going on. Please don't ever do that again."

Today when he tells that story, Len adds that it was very meaningful to him to learn that we were an ethical company, and that it wasn't acceptable to compromise yourself ever in any way. "It was very refreshing to hear that's *not* how business was conducted at Interstate Batteries," Len now says.

Employee Relations

Dealing with our employees was another area of responsibility that fell to Len Ruby. When it came to a termination, he says I pushed him to make sure it was necessary and that it was done right.

"Whenever you deal with employees," Len recalls me telling him, "make sure that you deal with them in a loving manner."

I've been asked if terminating people is hard for me to do, and how we do it at Interstate. The answer is: Since we pray like we do in our management meetings over all important matters (and letting someone go is a very important matter), we cover all the bases. We ask God to help us do the things we have to do that are best for each individual, so decisions like this are the result of a consensus that's been fully covered in prayer—usually over an extended period of time.

Every day we pray about our personnel situation, asking God to help us determine if we have people in the wrong spots and, if so, where to move them. If He wants us to move people out, or bring them in, or to use their gifts to the fullest in some other way, per His intentions, we want Him to make this known to us.

Interstate Batteries is often described by employees as being like a family. We've learned that good people beget good people, so we function contrary to a lot of what the graduate business schools advise. For example, they caution against hiring family members of existing employees, but we *do* hire husbands, wives, and other relatives. It's worked great for us!

We've also been asked how we hang on to good people so long. I would say it's because we have this "do unto others as we would have them do unto us" mentality, and that includes our employees. People, just by nature, gravitate to those people who treat them well. So if you treat people with respect and look after their best interests—pay them well, help them grow in their jobs, provide good benefits, offer them the prospect of a great career, encourage them to feel they are on a team—generally you receive back in kind. Plus, our company's been on a winning streak, so that helps!

Hiring Practices

Len recalls that when he first started we didn't have a personnel department. He told us this was a need that must be met. He was assigned to develop policies. He remembers how some of those policies came into being:

"One of the first people I hired was a young mother," he says.

Apparently I challenged him on that: "Is this what the Lord wants—that we take a young mother out of the home, away from her children? If we have choices, I want you to look very carefully at this," I told him. "If it's a single mother who really needs a job and has no choice but to work, I have no problem with that. Let's be very wise in our hiring practices."

Len says it took his thinking to a different level. He began to look at people differently, paying more attention to their overall needs. One of those people was Violet Vickery who started as our director of human resources. Violet, who was a neighbor to my brother Tommy, was a single mother. She was a dynamic person who has become a super manager for Interstate.

Helping people is about the most enjoyable thing I've discovered in life—even if sometimes you get a bloody nose. It's the right thing to do.

Violet had a very fine position in the banking business, but we recognized qualities in her that we desired in people for our management team. She was one of the first persons who came into the company without having had field experience or, as we so often said, "without having grown up in the company." According to the unspoken criteria at Interstate, Violet hadn't paid her dues.

Under her skillful leadership, though, screening, interviewing, and training of all prospective employees took place. Moreover, training of our distributors from all over the country began under her leadership. Violet tackled every challenge with gusto. She was another sovereign placement within the company.

Violet appreciates the creativity that is so evident in the multi-faceted people who are a part of our team. But she is quick to remind us that while it's great to have ideas, ideas in and of themselves—without hands and feet—are just butterflies that flit away.

"You've got to have people who are willing to take an idea, analyze it, work with it, and ask the hard questions. Will it work? Is it something that we need to do now, or is it something we put off until later?" she explains. "Not every idea is a good one."

I need to hear that every so often, since I am an idea person and some of my ideas have wings made of solid lead. Violet has helped me keep in mind that there has to be a real balance between my creativity and the practicality of a matter.

One of the Interstate programs I'm most proud of came about after I asked Len and Violet to see what they could do to help rehabilitate people. Their efforts led to a practice of bringing people in who have served time in prison or who have had drug problems. We have sought ways to help people work through their problems, relying on the wisdom and direction that God supplies. Some tough rehabilitation issues have been confronted along the way—we've had checks stolen and cashed, for example. But it's been worth it. Helping people is about the most enjoyable thing I've discovered in life—even if sometimes you get a bloody nose. It's the right thing to do.

LEADING BY EXAMPLE

9

Growing up I was basically lazy, so I decided early on that putting on a front is a lot of trouble and produces stress. Therefore people usually know where I stand on things. I'm pretty easy to read.

After I turned my life over to Christ, however, I soon recognized that if I was to lead by example, more than anything I would need wisdom and discernment. There was no way I could correctly lead a company such as ours without the Lord's leading. And that would take not only knowing God's Word, but also wisdom beyond what I possessed and the discernment that accompanies it. So I began praying for this gift—for that's what it is according to Proverbs: "For the LORD gives wisdom; / From His mouth come knowledge and understanding" (2:6).

Proverbs is the book of wisdom for life—here and now. I often read from the book of Proverbs. Since it has thirty-one chapters, you can go through it monthly, one chapter each day. I cannot tell you how much it has helped me, especially in business decisions and relationships.

Working on My Weaknesses

If I had a prayer of pulling off this company president thing, I knew I had to get to work on my weaknesses. I saw that the younger men were looking up to me as their mentor. I would have to lead by example.

In asking God for wisdom and discernment, He was faithful to point out to me—often through my brother Tommy and other coworkers—areas I needed to develop, improve, or change. For example, planning ahead more, or not procrastinating, or not getting too many irons in the fire.

"Become useful and helpful and kind to one another, tenderhearted . . . forgiving one another . . . as God in Christ forgave you."

Some of our men came in as singles. We saw them develop relationships with lovely young women whom they married (we were often there at their weddings), and then they started having kids. We always tried to care about the needs of every person in those young families.

I hoped our treatment of our employees would be a model and rub off on their treatment of others.

Take the distributors. In our business, distributors are our life-blood. I remember coaching one of our regional managers, Billy Norris, to respect our distributors and their opinions. But if Billy and others like him were to be respectful of others, they had to see it in me.

I have a tendency to be overly critical, especially of others, often not using the same standard for myself as I do for them. I've had to work on being more patient and understanding. There's a lot said in the Bible on that subject. Ephesians 4:32 stands out, and *The Amplified Bible* makes it so clear with these words: "Become useful and helpful and kind to one another, tenderhearted (compassionate, understanding, loving-hearted), forgiving one another [readily and freely], as God in Christ forgave you." Ouch! Those words have knocked the stuffin' out of my pride more than a few times.

Beat the Competition to the Punch

Rick Scarborough, one of our regional marketing managers, is another example of a young man who came to us in 1976 looking for his future. Rick says that was before I had gray hair and my trademark beard. He was an enthusiastic hard worker from the start, and we finally sent him out as a salesman. I told him to take four or five trips and then we'd look at how he was doing, call him back in, and take it from there. More than twenty years later we haven't called him back in, so I guess he did it right!

Today Rick makes ten to fifteen trips a year working with distributors in the United States. Under Rick's leadership a few years back, our sales group of national field men, area sales reps, phone power, and distributor personnel, opened over 25,000 new accounts in one year. Fantastic!

Rick and his team see their work as a game they have to stay on top of to beat the competition. They are winners who work hard and know how to play the game fairly and with integrity.

It pleases me to hear Rick say, "I try to mirror what you taught me, Norm—your beliefs and philosophy—and it works."

I only quote this to point out that when you've got men saying things like this, believe me, it keeps you on your toes. But we treat our people, our distributors and dealers, well—we provide perks that include NASCAR race trips, NFL training camps, our conventions, and things of this nature. These things definitely promote Interstate, but they are also personally enjoyable, which gives us all a little added benefit from our jobs.

A Struggle with Impatience

I'm not always as patient as I should be. In fact, to be downright honest, I have very little patience with instructions of how to put something together or figuring out anything that is mechanical. I discovered a long time ago, however, how to get around this. I play dumb. People who like that sort of thing will automatically take over. Then I don't have to take valuable time messin' with it, and I can target my energies and emotions on those things I know I can handle well. That's one of the advantages, of course, of being in the driver's seat.

When you are sort of a big picture kind of guy, little details, important as they are, can drive you nuts sometimes. My wife, Anne, has helped me greatly in recent years to understand a problem many people have but are not aware of. It's called Attention Deficit Disorder, or ADD. They say people like this are very intense. Do I have it? Maybe so.

For instance, Anne says that when she first married me she couldn't figure out why everything mattered so much to me. Little things that she thought were minor I could get intense over. One of the characteristics of persons with ADD is that they are intense about most everything.

Well, if I have ADD, it probably—overall—has been a plus in my life. Nobody has to tell me to get excited or pepped up about things that matter to me!

It's true, I'm not exactly slow paced! I tell myself, "Norm, don't major in the minors. Know what you do well, and concentrate on it. Most of the people who are a part of our Interstate team know that you have got to be in high gear much of the time, or you'll get left behind."

I drive my people crazy when it comes to getting ready for a convention or something in which I'm participating and there is some rehearsal required. I have no patience for rehearsals! Intellectually, I know they are necessary and important, but emotionally, I like to wing it. I just love the element of a sudden challenge. (It is definitely a challenge to work with me!)

Monkeys on My Back

My memory of myself from my earliest years, besides being lazy, is that I was a procrastinator. When it came to doing homework, I was every bit an undisciplined kid.

Actually, I did a pretty good job at the things I liked and enjoyed, but doing the other work was like pulling teeth. So, my tendency was to tackle the stuff I liked. But my mind told me that in order to succeed I had to do the other things too.

I taught myself to be responsible by "putting monkeys on my back" through the making of public commitments. I also struggled with a high level of pride (or maybe it's insecurity) and wanting to look good to others; so once I have committed to something publicly, my pride drives me to complete it as successfully as possible.

I tell myself, "Norm, don't major in the minors. Know what you do well, and concentrate on it."

Because of my leadership and high-profile position at Interstate, I've had to put myself more on the line. So I've had to become more disciplined. It's given me an incentive and motivation to be more responsible. I've had to learn to plan and then patiently plow the effort and assets I have into accomplishing what needs to be done.

"Plan your work and work your plan." I don't know who said it first, but the strategy produces successful accomplishments.

Choose Your Commitments

In athletics I was never really great at any one sport, but pretty good at some. If it came to the point of taking the "pretty good" and making it "great," which required repetition, discipline, hard work, and pain, I wouldn't do it.

Some of my attitude in sports carried over into my work habits. I had to fix that.

Now it's humorous to me that one of the key things I believe in with regard to business success—and life success—is tenacity! Tenacity, along with my high degree of competitiveness, has served me well.

The older I get, the better I am at making and living up to my commitments. The Bible has something to say on this. We are told that our yes should mean yes, and our no should mean no. We should never violate our word (James 5:12; Num. 30:2).

Commitments are not to be taken lightly, and when I make them, I need to honor my word—even when it may work out to my own detriment.

A man chooses his commitments. If I make a commitment, normally I'll just about die trying to keep it. So if I commit to somebody, where my reputation of being "a man of his word" is concerned, I normally will not let that activity go undone.

Achieving

I love achieving in something that I really believe in, those areas that have my interest and total commitment. As this relates to business success, I am convinced that a great percentage (maybe 80 percent) of the people that we at Interstate Batteries call on *need* and *want* our products and service—especially if they understand what we have to offer. We believe this is true, so not only are we achieving success by gaining their business, but we leave these people and their customers much better off than before we came.

If everyone who needs a battery can really get a better one from Interstate, then we want everyone to have an Interstate battery. This gives us both a special incentive and a commitment to get the job done.

Strategy and Creativity

By the time I became president of the company, I knew that money management in a business was extremely important. If you look at a range of people, probably one in five can handle money wisely. Just look at our country. Right now the American people, as a nation, are bankrupt. If everybody called our country's debts, individually and as a nation, we would come up short.

Because I don't relinquish important areas of authority easily, I decided that money wasn't one of the things our other folks at Interstate Batteries needed to be worried about. John Searcy had handled all the money decisions, and he had taught me a lot. The decision was made that my brother Tommy and I would handle finances. We had pretty good ability and exercised sound judgment more often than not.

The next consideration was personnel, including hiring and firing. I was the authority on that area, as I was on planning. I would ask for counsel from Tommy, Len, and Gene, but in the end, I made the decisions.

On people issues, I said to myself, "What you need to do, Norm, is just find people with good common sense . . . people who will work hard and will do what you lead them to do."

I got into an expediency mode: If I could make people's work simpler so they wouldn't have to be concerned about finances, personnel, and planning, then all they had to worry about was implementation.

So I sold everyone on trusting me, and then motivated them with the challenge of accomplishment and financial rewards. I also held them accountable. That may not have been how many business experts would have approached the situation, but the results are that we marched through "battery America" like Sherman marched through Atlanta.

But sometimes I would get going so fast it was like being caught up in a big wave. There would be a half dozen or so decisions that had to be made, and I'd be in the heat of something and might make three or four good decisions, but others could have been better. Plus, our business kept growing—more people, more projects, more battlefronts in the field. It got to where I couldn't keep up with it all. Yet my "system" involved me making most of the decisions.

I had key people and *their* people sitting and stymied, waiting on a decision from me. As you can well imagine, problems were the result. I realized that things couldn't continue like this, but I was somewhat confused, being in the stress of it all.

There is great value in listening to other people, especially when you know they are knowledgeable and listening to God. I learned that, like in a stew, the combination of the many produces more than just the sum of the individual parts. If you eat beef, potatoes, carrots, and tomatoes separately, they're good; but put them altogether in a stew with other savory ingredients and they are truly great. The right parts enhance the whole. It's the same with people management.

One day I read part of a book on business management from a biblically principled standpoint and my thinking was jolted. A major point was made in regard to the people of Babylon coming together and deciding to build a city and a tower into the heavens. God appraised their work and made this comment: "Behold, they are one people, and they all have the same language. And this is what they began to do, and now nothing which they purpose to do will be impossible for them" (Gen. 11:6).

There is great value in listening to other people, especially when you know they are knowledgeable and listening to God.

The book's author expressed how this Scripture offers much truth about how to accomplish things through people. God said they were one people (they were of one mind-set, unified, agreeing). They spoke the same language (they communicated, talked it out, made a plan, all understood each other). This was what they began to do (they were decided and committed, because they were doing it). The result was that nothing they purposed to do was impossible for them (from what they'd learned, they now could do anything they set their mind to doing). What a remarkable insight this was from God![1]

A light went on in my head as I took that illustration to heart. I'd always thought I was reasonably intelligent, but I couldn't understand how some individuals could come up with inventions like laser beams, televisions, jet engines—things that were totally incomprehensible to me. Then I got to thinking that most of these kinds of discoveries were the end result of group creativity—understanding and unity in strategy and planning of like minds, working together in commitment for years and years, personally and through writings often handed down.

The creativity of the masses is to be reckoned with. If God is our Creator and He has made us in His image, then our creativity is from Him. Man, what an incredible thought! But we are creative in many different ways and degrees.

So if you get a hundred people together, for instance, you can develop a broad spectrum of creativity, whereby they can zero in and focus on something. Then you can facilitate them in a direction they agree upon and commit to—a common goal.

You then work out a strategy to utilize the group's strengths and gifts to facilitate a plan. When we add a time frame and accountability to each other, and keep communicating where we are, how we are doing, and where we are going, we are getting real close to accomplishing whatever we purpose.

The realization finally swept over me that I'd been limiting the company because I had been relying on myself too much. With my brother, Len Ruby, and Gene Wooldridge, we decided who the top eight management people in the company were, and I met with them to share my thinking.

We brought in a management consultant, Jim Brewer, and together we all developed a new company mission statement, including a set of goals, priorities, and plans. We structured new departments and budget practices, giving others more authority, autonomy, and responsibility.

Plain and simple, I had seen that I was bogging everything down, because I insisted that everything clear through me. I wasn't able to cope with it all, and I was limiting the creativity and power of the company.

While Interstate Batteries had gained massive market share and obviously had been doing some things right, I had not been training management for the future.

I must admit, I had thrived on an expediency mode and the challenges it brought. I liked it that way. I liked calling all the shots and being actively involved in a participatory way. I got great fulfillment from doing things myself, as opposed to seeing them done through others. I had been the quarterback *and* the coach—Roger Staubach *and* Tom Landry! But it was now over, and rightly so.

Today we have a much stronger company based on the broad foundation of solid, talented professionals who work very hard to do their jobs the best they can.

Tommy and his team certainly deserve the credit for implementing our new management strategies. He became the CEO in 1991 and has not only set this new structure in place, but has also seen to it that we've broken the world record for the number of replacement batteries sold in one year (ten million), while increasing our account base to 200,000 businesses!

"Everything in its time," I always say. I was almost a little late on this sharing responsibility deal, but God spoke to me just in time. Or maybe I finally listened?

OVER BOULDERS AND AROUND HURDLES

10

When I began my walk as a Christian, I was really cranked up with enthusiasm and anxious to share what I was learning. It's so true that people do not know that God is really here, that He is relevant and meaningful for today! And what a difference He makes in our lives! I can attest to that and I have tried to tell others, although clumsily at times.

Mike Wier, now vice president of distributor acquisition and development for Interstate, was hired by me in August of 1973. He was twenty-one years old and had just come out of the Air Force.

During Mike's first year on the job, we made one road trip together that he refers to as his "springboard into the future." He was watching me more closely than I realized. I now had a new direction personally, having had my encounter with God. Faith had come into my life, and it was not a blue-eyed blonde. I was seeking to walk by faith in God, and I wanted others to experience what I had discovered.

I was giving Mike "double/triple doses of Scripture," in his words, and he was a captive audience, since we were sharing a hotel room together on this trip. As Mike says, "You were our company leader and everything you had to say was gospel, no pun intended, and I was all eyes and ears."

I was blazing a trail for Mike without realizing it. He was watching how I handled even the smallest of details, as well as the boulders and the hurdles. First impressions are often lasting impressions. Mike was wondering if work could be fun, if I was going to be down-to-earth and real, or if I would handle power and authority with arrogance.

I was supposed to be helping him with his selling on this trip, teaching him the ropes. Today Mike claims, "You were also helping me establish the foundation of my life, Jesus Christ—only I didn't know it at the time."

I had always been aggressive in making things happen, but now I needed to couple my bold aggressiveness with some sensitivity.

I didn't really know it either. I was hoping for this, but I can't say that I consciously understood how much God was working in Mike's mind and heart.

As we seek to live out our faith each day, we are, in effect, laying foundations and building on them as we relate to others. We can help others make, as Mike says, "some sense out of life—even when your own life is in turmoil, which it is at times, because real life is like that."

Mike is right. My life certainly has had its times of turmoil, yet I have tried to be stable, wise, and discerning. I had to take time for our people, recognizing that they, too, had turmoil in their personal lives. Often, they needed warm, honest friendship and had to know I cared about them before they would listen to me talk about the truth of Christ.

Sensitive Boldness

I was a very competitive salesman, and I was also going through some tremendous changes in my life when I began mentoring Mike. Trying to incorporate my new lifestyle into "on the road" reality, and walking the "straight and narrow," as Mike now describes it, presented challenges.

I wanted to influence this young man in the right way and to set the pace. I had always been aggressive in making things happen, but now I needed to couple my bold aggressiveness with some sensitivity. This required that I keep my focus where it belonged—on things that clearly pointed to the fact that my life was now directly related to this new relationship, this new faith I had with and in Christ.

"It appeared to me," Mike says, "that you had one thing on your agenda besides selling batteries, and it was to try and help people come into an understanding of what being 'saved' meant."

This can make a person unpopular with a lot of folks, but when you begin to share your faith, I've learned it should be with a sensible boldness, reinforced with prior prayer and tempered with a loving sensitivity.

Stepping Out in Faith

A big test of our management's willingness to step out in faith came when we first started talking about having a company convention. Our distributors began asking us why we weren't having conventions like our competitors, so this pressure pushed us into planning one.

We announced that our first Interstate convention was to be held in Maui, Hawaii, in April 1984, and that we would celebrate five million annual battery sales. Then the awakening came, as Len Ruby describes it. "What's going to happen? Is this something that we *really* want to start? We're going to bring all these distributors together. We know we have some problems—no company as large as ours is totally without challenges. Are we crazy or what?"

We were very negative at first about doing it—afraid to get our distributors all together, afraid that some negative attitudes would stir up the whole bunch, afraid our programs would be lousy. What did we know about giving a convention?

Whatever bad you could think of, we thought of it. It got so bad, this attitude of fear, that one day I got Tommy, Len, and Gene together and said, "Here's how I think we ought to handle this. We've got to pray about this convention every day."

So yes, of all things we resorted to prayer, and I mean *diligent* prayer. We were stepping out in faith, but it was pretty shaky faith. We made a prayer list of everything we wanted from the convention.

First, we asked God to bathe the entire time in the love of Christ. We asked that His love would be evident even to unbelievers, that we would all be like a loving family (those were our exact words), and that there would be *no* dissension—*none!* We asked God to reveal Himself through His love and that every person involved with the convention who wasn't a believer would come to the knowledge of the Truth. But we told God we didn't want to offend anyone, make people mad, or turn them off.

We prayed, too, about all the details and asked God to help us make this a successful event. Our prayer list included asking for safety, good weather, great meetings, fine speeches and presentations, and that the *entire week would be great fun.*

We began eighteen months out, praying together every workday morning for about twenty minutes or so.

"The Interstate Family"

Finally it was time for the convention. It was fantastic! Nine hundred attended, far more than we had hoped for. Every session was spectacular. Information the distributors needed to hear and retain was presented in bite-size portions. Vendors and other company participants in the trade show helped to make the program exciting. The distributors were entertained while still receiving practical information.

God answered our prayers! It was phenomenal. As a matter of fact, I'd never experienced anything like it before nor have I since. Without any prompting from us, our customers coined the phrase, "The Interstate Family," and told us, "There's something special here, a feeling of love, unity, family." The exact words of our prayers!

Now when we plan conventions, two years in advance, our planning group comes up with the creative ideas and presents them to senior management. Promo videos are sent to distributors well in advance to stir up excitement and enthusiasm. For example, before our Hawaii convention in 1992, management appeared on the promo video in hula skirts. It was hilarious! Then at the convention itself, the singing group of Tommy, Gene, Len, and myself, presented ourselves in lip sync with a big sound system as the Beach Boys on Waikiki Beach.

Our customers coined the phrase, "The Interstate Family," and told us, "There's something special here, a feeling of love, unity, family."

At another convention in Nashville, we presented ourselves as the backup group for Elvis, with Len Ruby in a flashy gold suit posing as the crooner. Len had to practice a lot to get the hip thing and the Elvis walk just right! The rest of us dressed in '50s tuxes and sang backup with choreographed dance steps like the rock 'n' roll groups of the good old days.

At Interstate we do believe in the value of humor. I agree with A. W. Tozer, the theologian, who wrote, "Your sense of humor doesn't have to dry up and die [because you're a Christian]. There's plenty to laugh at in the world—just be sure you don't laugh at that which God takes seriously, and conscience is one of those things." Our distributors have come to expect humor and the unexpected from us at the conventions, and we love doing it and watching them enjoy it.

Our company conventions have gotten bigger, with 2,300 in attendance in 1994 and even more expected in 1996. Our distributors say, "Interstate does it first class!" which is a nice compliment for all our people who work so hard to produce these memorable events.

Sunday Morning

When we scheduled the first convention dates, we purposely planned it over a weekend so that we could have a Sunday morning breakfast session as an official event of the convention. We felt this was wise in that no one probably would fault a "religious" message on a Sunday morning. After all, we *are* Americans! We decided to invite a speaker who could explain God's truth and offer Christ. We prayed that many would choose to believe in Christ.

At that first convention's Sunday morning session, Walt Hendrickson spoke and gave a dynamic gospel presentation, offering an invitation for people to accept Christ with "eyes closed and heads bowed." The people were so moved by this that afterward they applauded wildly.

Later, out by the pool, I was talking to a young man in his twenties from Houston and asked him, "What did you think of the speech this morning?"

"Hey, I thought that guy was really great! But he got a little *religious* there at the end!"

This young man definitely was not ready to respond to the invitation, but he wasn't offended either, which was a direct answer to our prayers. Most important, Christ was glorified and some folks were born anew and witnessed to.

This Sunday session is now a traditional part of our convention planning, and each time we invite a special speaker with name recognition, someone we know our attendees will appreciate and enjoy. Our speakers have included Chuck Colson, Tom Landry, Joe Gibbs, Jack and Jeff Kemp, and Mike Ditka.

A Battery Convention or a Revival?

Mike Wier said of this Hawaii convention that it was one of the most inspirational moments he's ever experienced with the company or with anyone. "You couldn't tell whether it was a battery convention or a revival!"

It took Mike ten years to make the decision to turn his life over completely to Christ. "What goes on *inside* the convention hall is more important than the location," he adds, recalling what took place in his own life.

The benefits of these conventions spill over into the interaction the distributors continue to have with each other long after the event is history and a pleasant memory. They call each other, ask for advice, and share ideas that work. The conventions have built strong friendships and have opened lines of communication more than anything.

All Because of Dedicating Ourselves to Prayer

After we saw the results of that first convention, we knew it was because we had dedicated ourselves to prayer; God had blessed and honored our actions.

Over the years, as leaders of the company, we had committed the business to God, asking for His counsel on how to run Interstate. So even before we had a personnel department and before the company was organized as it is today, we were pray-ers.

Today our executive team has a prayer time every morning. Our company chaplain, Jim Cote, joins them. Not everyone can make it every morning, but a nucleus is always there.

We've learned how to use prayer to go over the boulders and around the hurdles. Tozer says that prayer will increase in power and reality as we repudiate all pretense and learn to be utterly honest before God, as well as before men. I certainly have found this to be true for us.

CREATING NATIONAL AWARENESS

11

To help establish Interstate as a major player in the battery business, our first national advertising campaign was initiated in 1982 on Paul Harvey's radio show. Up until John Searcy's retirement in 1978, we hadn't ventured into this venue, but consumer awareness was growing. Automotive people kept hearing good things about Interstate Batteries, so we knew it was time to add national awareness to our company.

We looked at the amount of money we had and saw that we could do well in radio with what we were able to invest at that time. We weren't ready for TV. We picked what we felt was the best national radio program going and stayed with the *Paul Harvey News and Commentary* program for ten years.

It was the right choice, and today we're still known by many people as "Paul Harvey's batteries." The Paul Harvey persona put Interstate on the map in the minds of consumers by linking a virtual unknown (Interstate) with an internationally known and respected celebrity. We're forever grateful to Paul for going far beyond our contract agreement in promoting the Interstate name.

After our positive start with Harvey, we felt we were ready for other forms of advertising, one of which came to include part ownership/sponsorship of The Great American Race—the world's richest "old car" race, which runs from coast to coast in North America. The race appeals to race fans and vintage car lovers alike throughout the world. Also, as I described earlier, we became a part of NASCAR racing, which eventually led to the Interstate Batteries/Joe Gibbs Winston Cup racing team. In addition to that fantastic win at the Daytona 500 in 1993, our driver at the time, Dale Jarrett, won the Mello Yellow 500 in Charlotte, North Carolina, in 1994. In 1995 our racing success was even better with our great young driver, Bobby Labonte, who won three races. Bobby finished sixth on the money won list and tenth in the season's point standings.

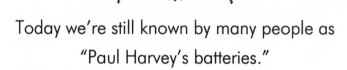

Today we're still known by many people as "Paul Harvey's batteries."

Besides these automobile competitions, we teamed in sponsorship with Steve DeSouza and Scott Gillman, Outboard Grand Prix race boat competitors, painting their boats the familiar Interstate green and black. It didn't take long before driver Steve DeSouza was Mercury Outboard Grand Prix National Championship runner-up (in 1993), as well as Scott Gillman (in 1994). We tailored our sales machinery to take advantage of their successes, and then we turned our high-voltage marketing team loose in the marine battery market.

Pure Americana: The Great American Race

In the early 1980s, as we found ourselves aiming for the top in national awareness, we began looking around for promotional events that would "play" well in small towns, as well as in larger cities. The Indianapolis 500 was the premier automotive event in America, and I thought it would be great if we could somehow get involved with it. But I knew at the time we didn't have the money to participate significantly.

With these thoughts kicking around in my mind, one day I received a call from a good buddy, Tom McRae, and we agreed to meet with our wives for dinner. He told me about something called The Great American Race, which was to run from Los Angeles to Indianapolis for $250,000 in prize money in May of 1983. But there was a catch: It was only for pre-World War II vehicles.

My ears perked up at the mention of Indianapolis. From Interstate's standpoint it looked like a good thing—the unique kind of promotional event I'd been hoping to find.

Tom and his friend Curtis Graf enjoyed "messin'" with cars, and Curtis had recently purchased about six thousand pounds of rust and assorted scrap iron, which was supposed to be a 1935 Twin-Six Packard. Curtis had convinced Tom to help him rebuild it so they could get into this Great American Race.

Tom's question to me was: "What do you think of the possibility of Interstate being a sponsor of our car? This race finishes in Indianapolis on the Friday night prior to the running of the Indy 500 on Sunday."

One thing led to another. To top it off, the original promoters of The Great American Race ran into all kinds of obstacles getting the race off the ground, and Interstate ended up not just being the sponsor of one old car, but, along with Tom, buying out the original race promoter. Whew, how's that for jumping in the ocean with your clothes on? But, of course, that decision wasn't made before I called in Tommy, Gene, and Len and had the original promoter make a presentation.

One day I asked Tom McRae how many cars he thought they'd have to have for a decent race. He told me at least twenty. There was a tremendous amount of risk involved—no one had ever done this before, and we would have to charge a five-thousand-dollar entry fee.

"How many people are going to step up and pay five grand?" we had to ask. "Will people *really* put these restored masterpieces out on the open road in competition?"

Next I asked what he figured it would cost for us to go out and buy or rent twenty old cars. This was a "worst-case scenario" because Curtis was the only entrant at that point. We pulled all the figures together, including the already advertised $250,000 in prize money. It looked like we could be out somewhere around $500,000 if the bottom fell out.

I looked at Tom and asked, "McRae, will this thing work?"

That was a very difficult question for Tom to answer. It stopped him cold. He describes it as "the point of no return." He and I had been friends for years, but we'd never had any business dealings together. The answer Tom provided suited me. "If God wants it to happen, it will work out."

That lighted my fire. I looked at him and responded, "That's right. And if *He* doesn't want it, we don't want it, right?"

Tom said, "Right!"

"Okay, let's pray about it," and we did, committing it to God. "We want to honor You, Lord, in all things. We are going to use our best intellect to go about doing this as a business venture, but if it isn't Your will, please stop it, close the doors, and don't let it happen."

I had told Tom I was busy and didn't want to start another business. It made more sense for Tom because he was looking for another career. So before we knew it, Tom and I were race promoters. Unfortunately, we didn't know the first thing about staging and promoting an old car race across the country. This was totally out of our hands. When we prayed and asked God to either close the doors or help us get on with this thing, we were dead serious. God took us at our word.

After that, it seemed before you could turn around, we were out one hundred thousand dollars in cash and had another hundred thousand due to hold hotel rooms in Indianapolis. This deal was going to be more risky than we'd planned.

So here it was, the end of January 1993, only about six months until The Great American Race. Nobody knew us or anything about any old car race. Interstate Batteries sure wasn't as well known as it is today. Rightfully so, people were asking, "Who are these guys in Texas saying they are going to pay a quarter of a million dollars in prize money for what they're calling 'The Great American Race'?"

I guess I was born a salesman—wearing a big smile and mouth a goin'!

The 150-pound tarpon that was an answer to a friend's prayer.

My family (l to r): my mother's mom (Idel), my father Lawrence, Jean, Jimmy, my mother Ruth, Janet. I'm the little guy in front of Dad, and Tommy is by my mom.

My mentor, John Searcy (center), with Tommy and me.

The Great American Race provided a tremendous public relations boost for Interstate Batteries. Here, Norm cuts a rug with Walt Disney's Minnie Mouse.

Joe Gibbs, crew, and me praying before Daytona.

"The Green Car"—the Interstate Batteries-sponsored Chevrolet Monte Carlo.

Joe Gibbs and I celebrate receiving our Daytona 500 rings.

Fellow Texan, George Bush.

Anne and me in Moscow.

A family meal during ministry outreach in St. Petersburg, Russia (l to r): me, Tommy's wife Scottie, Jim, Jim's wife Jean, Tommy, Anne.

Sharing the gospel is always a joy—in Mexico (above) and at a prison in South Carolina.

Our family in 1990 (l to r): Scott, Scott's wife Donna, me, Anne, Tracey.

My normal office pose—standing up while on the phone.

We mailed out some press releases and *slam dunk!*, a guy by the name of Leroy "Tex" Smith, then publisher of *Old Cars Weekly*, a publication for antique car enthusiasts, read the news release and hit a homer for us by running a front-page lead story. We received over three hundred phone calls that first week. Entries started rollin' in, and each one was cause for celebration.

"It's Gonna Be a *Great Race!*"

Today, Tom and I aren't quite as naive as we were back when we put together that first race. One day Tom called the man whom he'd been told was the Indy track official who really ran that show—Charlie Thompson. Tom asked about timing our race arrival in such a way that we could have a victory lap at Indy for our guys on the Friday of 500 week.

"No way!" Tom was told. He then called Jo Hauck, who was in charge of the 500 Festival Parade. She graciously thanked him for calling her, but assured him her parade was all set and didn't need any antique cars. But, being naive and persistent, Tom bulled ahead.

So here it was, the end of January 1993, only about six months until The Great American Race. Nobody knew us or anything about any old car race.

When Tom asked the Indianapolis police for a police escort, their response was the most colorful yet: "Man, you must be crazy! We'll have four hundred thousand wild fans in town, most of 'em drinking and partying. You ever been here on Indy weekend? My guys are working thirty-six-hour shifts, and if you bring those old cars into this town, you probably won't even get *through* town with the wheels left on 'em." And then he sounded a grim warning, "And if you *do* come, don't call us; we'll have our hands full!"

So much for our bright, original idea! Undaunted, Tom and I put our heads together and came up with another great idea: We needed to get actor Tony Curtis to drive in this race. We were recalling the movie that Tony had starred in, *The Great Race.* What if we could get him to be a spokesperson?

We didn't know it then, but Tony proved very hard to find. His agent couldn't even get a hold of him.

The whole race picture was looking rather grim. We checked to see if Los Angeles wanted to be involved. They couldn't have cared less. Indy had already let the air out of our tires. Entries were sluggish. And where on earth was Tony Curtis?

Somewhere along about that time, God started pushing the buttons. Watch out when that happens!

Tom's daughter, Sam, had a girlfriend by the name of Liz. Sam came home one night and said, "Dad, guess who Liz had dinner with last night?"

"Who?"

"Tony Curtis."

"Where?"

"In Spain!"

And then it hit Tom. "Tony Curtis? Did you say *Tony Curtis* is in *Spain?*"

And that's how we made contact with someone who had been so ellusive!

Then I came up with the name and number of Bob Wilds in Indianapolis, a Johnson Controls contact. (Johnson Controls is a major stockholder in Interstate, and they actually make the batteries under a special contract.) Bob Wilds turned out to be that special gift from heaven (and has since become a close friend) who got us the keys to Indy.

And Tony Curtis said to count him in too!

When these great things started happening, we knew God had dropped the green flag. Tom looked at me and said, "This is gonna be a great race!"

He was so right. The details all came together. God didn't just open doors, He blew them off the hinges with all the great stuff that happened! We were even welcomed like royalty in Indianapolis. But I need to tell more of the story first.

On the Road with the Great Race

I learned quickly that the rhythm of the Great Race was like running away and joining the circus. It's an adventure unlike any other. Every day, every hour, is an adventure of the best possible kind as the vintage cars with their proud owners rumble their way across the United States. Interstate Batteries is proud to be cofounders of such a challenging and exciting venture.

I'm happy to report that America is not what you see on the prime-time soaps. The real America is, fortunately, still out there and it's wonderful. It's incredible how the old cars blow away age, social barriers, and any need for formal introductions. Add the most important ingredient, the entourage of warm, outgoing, having-the-adventure-of-their-lifetime "Greatracers," as the racing teams are fondly called, and you've got a memorable event at every stop.

From the very beginning we made prayer a part of The Great Race. In the morning, at lunch, and at overnight stops we have prayer, asking the good Lord for the safety of racers and a blessing on that particular community or city. Proverbs 16:3 reminds us that when we commit our works to the Lord, our plans will be established. We wouldn't dream of not including God in our plans.

How the race operates is pretty interesting. Older cars receive what we call an "age factor handicap." The sliding handicap system works like this: A 1942 automobile, for instance, has an age factor of one thousand. A 1910 car's age factor is 0.614. If these two cars were to finish with a ten-second score (the lower the number of seconds, the better the score), the 1942 final score would be ten seconds; the 1910 vehicle will have a score that is ten seconds times its factor number of 0.614 rounded to the nearest second, or a score of six seconds.

Older vehicles do not have the reliability, roadability, and serviceability newer machines enjoy. The purpose of the age factor handicap is to level the playing field.

The drivers work very hard; the routes chosen are long, hard stretches. Racing street-legal antique cars 170 to 480-plus miles a day on back roads over all kinds of terrain during every kind of weather imaginable—it's a true contest with a goal other than speed. It's best described as a controlled-speed competition of precision driving and endurance. The smallest error or mechanical malfunction can ruin a team's chances.

From the very beginning we made prayer a part of The Great Race.

Greatracers hail from all age groups. You'll find husband and wife, father and son, brothers, and just good friends. The love of antique automobiles is both the lure that attracts them and the glue that seals them into a cohesive unit of a hundred or more participants each year.

These Greatracers attack today's roads and traffic with yesteryear's state-of-the-art machines, seeking to excel and win some of the big $250,000 prize money awarded in several different categories. Sometimes it's a jaunty journey of joy, but always a torturous exercise of skill, determination, and survival.

Spirit Is What It's All About

As the first race wound its way from Knott's Berry Farm in southern California all the way to Indianapolis, we were increasingly aware of how special this race was becoming. The event brought out the best in everyone. Additionally, this was excellent public relations for Interstate Batteries.

One great human interest story after another popped up. For example, at one point we were in Kansas City, right in front of the downtown Hilton Hotel. Tom Lester had his one-of-a-kind 1909 Mercedes (valued at more than one million dollars) parked out front with the hood up and his mechanic, Benny Kekline, working with him.

When I walked up, the lights of the car were on, and the men were pulling valves out of the engine, really thrashing on the car. It looked like that old Mercedes was going to be out of the running. This was the oldest car in the race, and the award for the "Oldest Car to Finish" competition was $25,000. It was a huge disappointment they faced, but they kept working away as I went on inside the hotel.

Later I found out what happened after that. Another driver, named Doc Fuson, and his bunch came by and got to talking to Lester.

"The valves are burned out," Lester told Doc. "We've got to have a machine shop grind the valves." Lester was an expert machinist by trade, but he needed a valve grinding machine to do that job.

Doc said, "I know a guy right here in town who's got a machine shop. Let me see if I can find him." To make a long story short, Doc called the guy at home, got him out of bed, the guy came down, opened up his machine shop, Doc took Lester to the shop, Lester ground the valves, came back, and fixed his Mercedes.

Lester said to Doc, "You know, you're crazy because this is going to cost you $25,000."

You see, Doc had the next oldest car, "Big Thunder," a 1910 American La France fire truck. Doc's reply was classic: "Well, you just haven't got my bill for services yet!"

But he helped him fix that vehicle, and yes, Lester went on to get the twenty-five grand, and the Doc came in second. Doc Fuson may have lost the big bucks, but he earned himself a chunk of Great Race legend with his selfless act.

We decided to give out a "Spirit of the Event" award each year, and the first winner was Dr. Robert "Doc" Fuson of Warsaw, Indiana. The award is now called the "Doc Fuson Spirit of the Event" trophy.

Checkered Flag

Yes, we all finally made it to Indianapolis. When we arrived the Friday before the Indy 500, Indy's thirty-two-officer World Champion Motorcycle Drill Team shut down drive-time traffic and escorted our Greatracers to the Indy 500 track for a victory lap, then through downtown, around Monument Circle, and on to our hotel.

Out of the sixty-nine cars that had started in the race seven days before, sixty-two were still running strong!

Sixteen of our cars joined the Indy Festival Parade on Saturday, and Tony Curtis, an old friend by now, was featured along with our race winner in a special victory lap around the world-famous brickyard. The first Interstate Batteries Great American Race had roared from nowhere into national prominence.

It has turned out to be a very colorful, pure Americana, cross-country event with flags waving, the U.S. Navy band participating, and other sponsors such as American Airlines, GoodYear, Featherlite Trailers, Chevy Trucks, Buick Motor Division, and MBNA America Bank.

Originally declared "impossible" and "absolutely crazy," the Interstate Batteries Great American Race has sent its critics to the pits and earned its pole position in vintage-car racing. The race has helped put Interstate Batteries on the nation's map.

And I am absolutely convinced that God gave us the race.

TO FINISH IS
TO WIN

12

Although that first Great American Race was an advertising grand slam for Interstate Batteries, the race itself was rather rugged. Try driving up to 350 miles a day through the heat and rain in an old car that has no air-conditioning or power steering or power brakes! Over the years experience has taught us a lot, so we've adjusted the race rules and made other changes.

One of the things that didn't change, though, was the crowds that turned out to greet us along the way, as we made our lunch stops, pit stops, and overnight stops. We were hosted and feted by hundreds of towns and millions of wonderful people during the thirteen races that we sponsored.

During the first Great Race in 1983 we realized early on that the sight of old cars winding through the back roads was striking a chord with a broad spectrum of Americans. Perhaps the biggest surprise was how excited entire communities became. There are many special memories, including those of a town named Booneville, Missouri, which the race passed through the day before the finish in Indianapolis. Booneville is a small town, typical of the hundreds of little towns that were to welcome us over the years. There was a man named Jack Palmer who kept calling and telling us the race just *had* to come through Booneville. So we altered our course just a little and included Booneville.

It was great! As we drove into town we saw posters on telephone poles—grade-schoolers had made them—that said "Welcome Racers!" They were everywhere! We drove by retirement homes, and the people there were all out on the front lawn parked in their wheelchairs.

Everywhere we looked we saw flags waving. The high school band was playing on the courthouse lawn. It was a big deal for the whole community, and there were more people there than lived in the county, we were told.

And the food! Fresh lemonade, old-fashioned hamburgers with all the trimmings grilled by the local citizens on their grills in the town square, homemade ice cream, and cookies—a feast like you've never quite seen!

There was a man named Jack Palmer who kept calling and telling us the race just had to come through Booneville.

The dining on these trips is spectacular. We've had some of the best food a hungry racer could ever hope to eat in towns all across America. Sometimes it's old-fashioned strawberries and shortcake; often it's barbecue or finger-lickin' chicken or hot dogs. No matter what part of the country we're in, the food is usually good ol' home cookin'.

In 1988, at another town—Salina, Kansas—we were blown away with the magic they created with their "The Wizard of Ahs" promotion.

Salina has brick streets. Right where the Greatracers came in the good citizens had painted Main Street gold—just like the yellow brick road in *The Wizard of Oz*. A huge arch had been built where the cars turned onto Main Street and drove down the yellow brick road. They had gotten some dry ice and fans were blowing so that the arch poked through the clouds. What a sight!

Since a different route for the race is chosen each year, a new following of admirers comes into existence with greater national awareness. You can be sure of lots of handshakin', backslappin', good food, hospitality, prizes, and surprises in community after community. And that's the way it is each year all across America. The Great American Race is an ongoing celebration of good ol' American hospitality.

No Place for Wimps

The race has certainly grown since that first year when we had six staff cars accompanying the entourage. In later years, Buick supplied us with thirty-seven staff cars and Chevy supplied ten trucks. Our staff, operational people, television crews, a media headquarters van, and the Featherlite trailers (producers of the best utility trailers in the business) all headed out. We had a headquarters trailer and a merchandising trailer with T-shirts, hats, pins, yearbooks, and all kinds of paraphernalia. We took two crews of college kids to sell yearbooks at the stops (they get to see the country in this trip-of-a-lifetime across America and make some money to help with college expenses).

The entourage fluctuates each year with between six and eight hundred people, including the U.S. Navy Ceremonial Band. The band heralds Greatracer arrivals at lunch and overnight stops and performs twilight concerts at overnights.

Details, Details, Details

Here's how The Great American Race all comes together. Staff experts log over 20,000 miles on three trips each year across the U.S. to find the most challenging back roads for the competition. Interstates are used sparingly (the highways, not the batteries!). We use only about 10 percent of the interstate system across the country, mainly to enter and leave cities.

Because the race rolls on back roads, you'll often see old-timers standing there, looking at the old cars with tears running down their faces. It brings back so many memories for them. And you'll see little kids and young people looking on in awe. Sure, you can see some of these cars in museums, but they just sit there, locked up and dead. What the Great Race does is to take artwork off the wall, so to speak, and bring it to life, out there on the road doing what it was meant to do.

Each speed change, stop, start, and turn is detailed meticulously in driving instructions, measured to within one-hundredth of a mile. Exact speeds and "perfect" drive times are allotted for each maneuver. The object of the race is to match these "perfect" times (unknown to the racer). To make it even tougher, no electronic devices are allowed in the cars and odometers are removed or sealed.

Thirty minutes before each day's start, teams (consisting of two people—the driver and the navigator) pick up driving instructions that tell them what to do and where to go until the finish that night. These directions are accurate to within one-hundredth of a second. Racers may use only a time-of-day clock, an analog stopwatch, a speedometer, and pencil and paper. That's all.

Following directions and doing calculations are hard enough. But to add insult to injury, Greatracers must function almost perfectly while driving fractious antique cars whose designers never dreamed they would *ever* be asked to cross the U.S.

Several times daily, each team's progress is checked at secret checkpoints by video cameras with electronic timer/printers, then sent to central scoring via satellite. Each second off schedule is a penalty point.

For instance, in 1991, one team was just one second away from "perfect" for a 350-mile day. Scores with five- to ten-seconds' error for the day are not uncommon.

The Numbers

The Interstate Batteries Great American Race has been described as a kaleidoscope of numbers—fourteen days; sixteen states; forty-seven stops; 4,250 miles; up to one hundred race cars, with almost 250 vehicles all told (Greatracer friends and families); 6,800 hotel rooms;

over 25,000 breakfasts, lunches, and dinners; and over one million race miles traveled. Moreover, more than 50,000 gallons of fuel are burned, with hundreds of thousands of spectators along the roadsides and thousands more watching via the media.

The event is always covered by the most prestigious news and entertainment broadcasters and print media in America, including an ESPN one-hour special, ABC's *Good Morning America,* NBC and CBS television and radio networks, CNN, *USA Today, The Los Angeles Times,* United Press International, Paul Harvey, the Mutual Broadcasting Network, and Unistar.

Obviously, our goal of gaining national attention for our green and white batteries has been greatly aided by this race, which began so innocently one night over dinner with friends.

The question is: What do you do when you're number one? The answer is: Stay there! And that's what is happening.

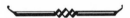

The message received across America was that we were a company that provided a top-quality product with a unique service infrastructure; the result was an expanding IBSA customer base. Before we knew it, other companies saw Interstate Batteries Great American Race's strong advertising and marketing potential and hopped aboard.

Two Dreams Combined

In 1983, when the Great American Race was just a dream in the making, I had another dream already in the works: the goal to make Interstate batteries America's number one replacement battery. The two dreams combined and grew—the Great Race into America's premier old car race and Interstate into America's number one replacement battery. The question is: What do you do when you're number one? The answer is: Stay there! And that's what is happening.

Interstate batteries carry the slogan "Built to Last." This carries over into our lives—there's going to be lots more racing history to be made, Lord willing, in the years ahead. But for some of us, the "great race" has more to do with life itself—not antique cars. We're headed into an eternity that will last forever, and our prayer is that we can be instrumental in helping others discover what the great race of life is really about.

> Therefore, since we have so great a cloud of witnesses surrounding us, let us also lay aside every encumbrance, and the sin which so easily entangles us, and let us run with endurance the race that is set before us, fixing our eyes on Jesus, the author and perfecter of faith, who for the joy set before Him endured the cross, despising the shame, and has sat down at the right hand of the throne of God. (Heb. 12:1-2)

To finish is to win.

PART THREE
Don't Just Stand There . . .
Do Something!

EXPANDED HORIZONS

13

When I became a Christian and my life changed so radically, I began to think a lot about what impact my faith should have on the job. Obviously, I was not in a position to make major changes at Interstate Batteries because my boss, John Searcy, set policy and was in charge. John had very high standards and set a tremendous example. But I wondered just what the possibilities might be to make more Bible-based beliefs an even greater part of the business.

When John retired I was in a position to try some things. I prayed about how we might proclaim Christ to all our employees, and to our customers as well. I wanted everyone to experience God's great love and forgiveness.

One day I spoke to my brother Tommy and Gene Wooldridge about us stepping out more in faithfully sharing the truth of Christ. "Can personal ministry be the bottom line in business?" I asked them.

We began praying about this issue and God led us to start trying a few things. I became more vocal about my faith and the spiritual dimension of the company. As Interstate grew and prospered over the next few years, more and more ministry-related telephone calls and letters started coming in, along with many prayer requests. Invitations for me to attend dinners and meetings increased to the point where I couldn't keep up. It became obvious that the needs we were surfacing called for a chaplain-type individual who could help me make wise decisions in regard to handling our contributions, as well as help properly organize everything and in ministering to company employees.

After trying a couple of part-time fellas, along came a young man named Jim Cote. He and I attended the same church, and Jim had a good track record in his own small business, as well as an extensive knowledge of the Scripture. But even more than that, he and his wife, Brenda, and their three boys each had an excellent reputation of trying to live their lives each day to honor God.

I explained to Jim that my life had taken on a new meaning when I gave it to Christ, and that most of my earlier motivation to succeed had been fear of failure; I had driven myself so as not to fall behind my peers. I was always working and striving to win, afraid that everyone was going to beat me. But when I gave my life to Christ—for Him to make of me what He wanted—I was set free from fear of business failure. I told Jim, "It's been a wonderful freedom to be able to just try to do my best in life and not have to worry about the result of what I'm doing, and not be driven by the compulsion of fear of failure."

Putting oneself in God's hands is real freedom. As author and speaker Josh McDowell has said, "Most people know what they ought to do, but they don't have the power to do it. They're in bondage." Christ is the bondage-breaker.

Jim and I hit it off and he picked up quickly on what was on my heart—that the bottom line of Interstate was to love people and try to meet their needs, all in the context of top performance and reasonable profitability. I told him we'd decided that we were going to live for and share the truth of Christ in our business, and the decision had been made some years before not to fear that this might in some way bring harmful repercussions.

Although I really wanted to share God's truth with people, I didn't want us to run over anyone or come off as being righteously obnoxious. We always ask God to help us be sensitive and kind, not ever desiring to offend anyone, but at the same time to be appropriately bold and obedient to share His love with others as He would lead us.

It didn't take long before I could tell that Jim Cote could give us the help we'd been looking for, and we asked him to join Interstate as our full-time contributions coordinator and company chaplain.

Putting oneself in God's hands is real freedom.

"In some respects," I told Jim, "I feel like the patriarch of Interstate in that I have a responsibility to all these folks and their families to share what I have experienced and to look out for their best interests to the extent that I can; but I recognize that my personal ministry can extend only so far." I had studied the Old Testament passages concerning Abram being the leader of many families (later his name was changed to Abraham), and I identified with him somewhat.

I needed to bring Jim up to speed on how our commitment to operate in a Christlike manner had worked itself out so far. I shared with him that we prayed at all food functions with our employees and distributors and that we sent our distributors cards with a meaningful Christian greeting at holidays. On occasion we also sent them books or special messages when there was sickness or a death in the family.

I told Jim, "We've put the message of Christ out before our employees and distributors in a sensitive manner, not trying to cram anything down someone's throat. But also we haven't stopped short because of some intimidation that maybe we shouldn't be sharing God's love. We've put our faith in God's hands."

So Jim came on board and became a partner in our personal ministry within the corporate setting. And in turn, Jim has employed students from nearby Dallas Theological Seminary to assist him part-time in our efforts.

Jim is a great facilitator of management's ideas—especially ideas on how best to minister to people. His strength lies in conceptualizing ideas. He claims I have an idea a minute. When I present one of those ideas to him, he sees it, we figure out what it's going to take to make it happen, develop the idea, and then he runs with it. Everybody should have a blessing like Jim Cote!

The Interstate Batteries Chaplaincy Program

As our company chaplain, Jim and his team facilitate pastoral ministry for the company and some of our distributors. Jim also helps manage the giving aspects and our missionary/ministry support as contributions coordinator.

At any given time, we may have three or four after- or before-work Bible studies going. We have a "Pizza Thursday" each month when we bring in Christ-centered speakers, such as Leighton Ford, Luis Palau, Chuck Colson, Bill Glass, Don Campbell, Howard Hendricks, or Tony Evans. Interstate buys the pizza, the employees can invite their friends or family members, and we average a hundred or so at each luncheon.

There is also a monthly birthday luncheon where Interstate provides the food and we celebrate employee birthdays for that month.

At corporate headquarters we have as many as a hundred people—our volunteer "prayees"—using prayer cards provided by the chaplain's department to pray for our missionaries and people whom we support.

Some Interstate Batteries' employees have even taken missions trips through a program we started in 1989. These volunteer trips give our people an exposure to missionary projects we support, including ones in Monterrey and Mexico City in Mexico. The company shares the expenses. Working with Global Missions Fellowship (GMF), we go door-to-door and do personal evangelism, and we also show the *Jesus* film through Campus Crusade for Christ.

In Dallas we often sponsor two or three tables to various missions banquets and breakfast events and provide tickets to our employees to encourage them to attend. In particular, we learned that events featuring well-known athletes and coaches were the most desired. We could count on a big turnout and our people would use the tickets.

We celebrate the President's National Prayer Breakfast with our employees, holding our breakfast on the same day as the one in Washington each year.

Our E-mail prayer chain is monitored by many employees. Urgent prayer requests for employees, their families, our distributors, and their customers are put on the computer as they come in, and we pray for each other.

We've also been praying more than seven years for all our dealers and their employees and families, for each one to receive Christ and come to the knowledge of the truth. With over 200,000 dealers—plus *their* employees and families—we figure this comes to several million folks who are being prayed for.

We always have our eyes peeled for appropriate material to send out. For instance, several years ago God gave us connections with a new Christmas music tape by Word Publishers, *Our Christmas,* featuring Sandi Patty, Michael W. Smith, Amy Grant, and other outstanding musicians. We mailed the tape and a little tract to all our distributors and dealers. Over 200,000 of each were sent out!

The tract offered salvation in Christ and assurance of His help so anyone struggling with a compulsion—alcohol, drugs, pornography, whatever—could discover how to be set free. It was entitled *The Gift of Freedom . . . and Power for Living.* It proved to be a kind of watershed. I'm thankful it was well received by the recipients, with hundreds of positive responses compared to only a few negative reactions.

This showed us something meaningful about being a witness for Christ in the marketplace. People really do need God's love, hope, and encouragement. But we always pray to be sensitive in what we say and do.

We've given away (and continue to give away) hundreds of Bibles to distributors and their employees, as well as to the people at the Interstate corporate office. All new employees receive a Bible on their first day of work.

One time we sent our distributors a memo about three great

Christian books to help them in understanding and raising adolescent children. It's been thrilling to give out hundreds of such books that we know will benefit our Interstate family.

At headquarters we also have a large library, and all employees have access to Christian tapes, books, videos, and magazines that they can check out through the chaplain's office. This is the VCR generation, so our video library is the most used. When employees tell us what they'd like to see, we try to get it for them—videos that will be helpful to them personally and to their families, or ones that provide good, wholesome entertainment. When employees come and say they have encountered some kind of problem or are looking for something special, Mary McDufee (Jim Cote's secretary) knows just the right material to place in their hands.

With over 200,000 dealers—plus their employees and families—we figure this comes to several million folks who are being prayed for.

Our chaplain is available for "light" counseling, and we are prepared to make referrals for "heavy" problems (alcohol and drug addiction) to professionals.

The response to the chaplain program has been phenomenal and sometimes surprising. Once, in a one-month period, Jim Cote even performed a marriage and a funeral along with his other duties. We certainly don't attempt to take the place of a church, but many people today just don't have any family or pastoral connections. So we try to encourage them and be there for spiritual help when needed. Then we will work with them to find a church home and other people who care.

Jim helped for two years in the development of a chaplaincy ministry for the International Outboard Grand Prix (IOGP). Our driver, Steve DeSouza, came to Christ through his relationship with Interstate.

Later, he and his wife, Missy, played the leading role in supplying speakers for IOGP services on Sunday mornings before the races. Lyle Blackwood, a former professional football player who works in our distributor recruiting area, was also instrumental in keeping this ministry going. Another ministry we support, Motor Racing Outreach (MRO), has since taken over this outreach to boat racers as an arm of their work. MRO is widely known for its wonderful ministry to the NASCAR teams constituency.

Our efforts to reach out for Christ do not stop with our employees and distributors. A duplicate of the Interstate Batteries race car, the green #18 Monte Carlo, is used in various settings to draw crowds and promote the company (including going into prisons all over America as a part of the Bill Glass Prison Ministry). When the car is displayed, we distribute a pamphlet that tells about NASCAR racing and also includes an evangelistic message by Joe Gibbs. Every time the car goes out, the pamphlet goes too as a personal souvenir for the onlookers. The pamphlet is also handed out at races and at our sportswear trailer (which sells souvenirs at every Winston Cup race nationwide).

We've also mailed to every one of our dealers a forty-minute video presentation of Joe Gibbs's life—his failures and his successes. It's basically his testimony to God's salvation and goodness in his life. The response to this has been very positive.

Chaplain Jim Cote, along with seminary students working for Interstate, has gone into the neighborhoods of Dallas to do door-to-door evangelism with materials printed in both English and Spanish. To date, they have introduced more than 150 people to Christ. Once these people have given their lives to the Lord, we find a compatible, cooperative church home for them that will try to integrate these new believers into their fellowship.

Marriage and the Road

One of the things we have done that has brought a tremendous response and a lot of satisfaction to all of us at Interstate is develop a twelve-part booklet and video series called "Marriage and the Road."

I was talking with Jim Cote one day and mentioned that I wanted to do something special to help our national field men. These men really represented the lifeblood of the company, because they were traveling out there, selling batteries all over the country, often away from their families for as many as twenty-one weeks out of the year. I've always been very conscious of the fact that the men who took this company to the front were these national salesmen.

I also remembered only too well my own days out on the road away from my wife and children, so I had perspective on what could possibly be going on in some of their marriages. I wanted to develop a means of encouraging them—to give some needed tools that would actually enhance their marriages, even with the travel separation.

My contention is that God's mandate to love is more important in business than just the business itself.

I asked Jim to come up with some material that would specifically address marriage/family issues as they related to salesmen on the road. He went back to the drawing board and called a contact (author Bill Hendricks) who was familiar with both marriage- and business-related issues. Bill Hendricks had access to data banks, but after searching everywhere, he couldn't find anything—written, audio, or visual—that related to marriage and traveling salespeople.

Bill and Jim got together and decided that a video program would work best with this group. The field men themselves and their wives were contacted and asked what the core issues were that they struggled with in their marriages. Then, at an Interstate Batteries picnic, Jim went armed with some open-ended questions, and he casually began to ask a few couples about their feelings regarding travel stress. Within fifteen minutes he had created a near riot. A crowd gathered, and everyone wanted to get in on the act. We knew we'd hit a nerve!

Bill went to work on isolating issues that had repeated themselves in preliminary questioning, and we settled on a dozen major issues. We decided on an interview format with Jim conducting the interviews, along with Howard and Jeanne Hendricks, Bill's parents, responding to what the couples revealed. Both Howard and Jeanne are noted authors and worldwide speakers on marriage and family issues.

When the twelve videos were finished we felt like we had a blockbuster (no pun intended), and time has proven we were correct in feeling that way. Companion study materials were developed so each couple would have "homework." Part of these exercises were developed to be done together when the husband is home, while the others are done individually.

Creating the "Marriage and the Road" videos and booklets has communicated to our field families how strongly we support them in the home. Spiritually speaking, we felt the Lord was leading us in this project all the way.

We've had requests from other corporations and ministries for the "Marriage and the Road" video series and are pleased with its expanded use.

The success of the videos went beyond our expectations, and we kept hearing, "What's next?" There was no way we could do an encore for this project, but Jim did come up with the idea of a monthly newsletter with the same title. It has also become enormously successful.

A Twenty-Four-Hour-a-Day Deal

Some say the business world is dog-eat-dog, and you can't make it if you don't play the game that way. Interstate Batteries is testimony that that's not true. We pray and try to honor God in what we do, and His blessings are quite evident.

My contention is that God's mandate to love is more important in business than just the business itself. If it seems that profits conflict with our obeying God, we try to obey God. Of course, we're not perfect by a long shot, and we often fall short. But we aim and try.

I only want whatever God wants me to have. If our horizons

continue to expand and we are given more opportunities to love and obey God, we will continue to give thanks and try to always honor Him and His Word. That's the only way I want to do business!

ULTIMATE INVESTING

14

Becoming a person of faith brought about a transformation not only of my personhood, but also of my principles concerning the management of money. One of the things my business experience had taught me was the wisdom in making good investments.

When I read a passage from Scripture I realized how foolishly I had invested the first thirty-five years of my life:

> *Do not lay up for yourselves treasures upon earth, where moth and rust destroy, and where thieves break in and steal. But lay up for yourselves treasures in heaven, where neither moth nor rust destroys, and where thieves do not break in or steal; for where your treasure is, there will your heart be also. (Matt. 6:19-21)*

I knew that I wouldn't deliberately throw money away, yet that's exactly what I'd done with my life for so many years.

Anne and I were seeking to put God's interests first in every aspect of our personal lives, and now I wanted to be sure I had brought that mentality with me into the corporate world—doing things the right way, God's way, with all the resources that ultimately belonged to Him anyway.

Because I was so blessed in being grounded in the truth of the Bible, the principles regarding giving became fixed in my thinking. As God's Word says it, I believe it. Therefore, I have always felt the responsibility to be a good steward of one's money. "It is required of stewards that one be found trustworthy" (1 Cor. 4:2). *The Amplified Bible* version of that verse says "Moreover, it is [essentially] required of stewards that a man should be found faithful [proving himself worthy of trust]."

I like to think of giving in terms of "investing," because I am oriented toward getting the best value possible for every nickel I spend.

Early on in my executive career I learned that many corporations give money to various charities—with almost all of it going to secular organizations. So as time went on, Interstate began giving also, but with over 95 percent of the money going to Christian ministries. We decided that with most businesses supporting other causes, we would direct our giving to Christian efforts and this became a major prayer priority.

Becoming a person of faith brought about a transformation not only of my personhood, but also of my principles concerning management of money.

With the enormous number of requests we were fielding, it was necessary for us to develop something that would aid us in making wise investment decisions to enhance our stewardship of that which had been entrusted to us. In order to create objectivity in the giving process, Jim Cote and I developed a grid for giving that we call MUSIG (which is not *music* misspelled!). Each letter stands for a measuring standard used to determine whether or not we should give to a particular project.

Someone has said that those requesting help from us have to "face the MUSIG," which is quite true. A look at what those letters represent follows:

M stands for multiplication. If the most important response in life is to love God and others, the most loving act in life is to provide others with the opportunity to come to know God. This puts the multiplication of the truth of how each person can have a new and eternal life through belief in Jesus Christ as number one on our list in evaluating spiritual investments.

To pass this test on our grid, a request for funding must show how the proposed effort will multiply the number of people who will hear the truth of Christ, as well as the number of people who will be trained to carry it to others. It is not enough just to tell others about Jesus for us to invest in a ministry. There must also be the intention and capability to reproduce reproducers—to build the new believers so they can take the message to others who have not yet heard or responded.

An example of this is the university ministry of Campus Crusade in which many transferable concepts are used to train both old and new believers in reaching others.

U stands for urgency. A strategy for multiplication is number one, but the urgency of the opportunity is also very significant. For example, the intense spiritual responsiveness in the former Soviet Union pushed that nation to the top of our giving list. We had to ask, Is it an urgent situation? How much time do we have in the Confederation of Independent States in comparison to other parts of the world? Or, is there a part of the world that may not represent as great an opportunity but, due to war or economic collapse or spiritual opposition, its priority needs to be higher due to the urgency of the situation?

S stands for scope. Some situations offer a very focused opportunity for urgent multiplication, whereas others have these characteristics but also have a larger scope. A broader scope to me, as a businessman, represents a better spiritual investment for the long term.

This point of view isn't true for everyone, of course. Some people have specific interests because of their cultural background, personal pilgrimage, or some other influence where God directs attention to a particular need. I certainly embrace that, but scope is also important to us when evaluating opportunities.

Scope also speaks to how large a potential for impact the venture has. A ministry that is focused in one specific individual toward a particular geographical setting may have great multiplication potential, but its scope could be quite narrow. Since there's only one individual and the ministry is unique to him or her, the skills cannot easily be reproduced.

To us an example of an opportunity having great scope is the *Jesus* film project. The *Jesus* film teams employ ongoing, transferable processes and have a much broader impact (worldwide) than any single individual could ever have. We think this makes them a good spiritual investment for us.

I stands for impact. Impact deals with the issue of timing and efficiency, and with the management of the organization involved. How long will the money be tied up? How rapidly will the project get to the action stage? How much of the funding will be used for administrative overhead compared to how much will get to the front lines? How efficient is the organization overall in managing its vision and its resources? What is the group planning to do in the next year that shows them to be worthy recipients of the money?

Questions such as these on impact must be asked before we release money, not only because this is good stewardship but because giving, we think, should be done without the intent to control. One of the key thoughts contained in the biblical command that those with the gift of giving should give generously is that they give without attempting to control or to buy influence. It is not the giver's responsibility to co-opt the vision of an organization but to help accomplish it.

It is our position that if we, as givers, cannot release the money without concern, then the funds should be directed to another opportunity. However, we do feel we have the right and responsibility, as good stewards, to establish accountability standards in accordance with the agreed-to and intended purposes. To expect and receive reports of the impact of the gift are both appropriate on the part of the receiving organization and an encouragement to us.

G stands for growth. Growth relates primarily to the ministry venture's potential to be duplicated. If it is tied primarily to one event or a specific personality, then it may not be easily reproducible, which could mean that growth will be slow or impossible.

We like to choose ministries that not only fulfill their immediate objectives as presented, but also those that can successfully be duplicated in other situations. A secular example of such growth would be the McDonald's restaurant chain that has been established in every setting imaginable, from urban centers to suburban shopping strips to interstate highway exits to airports—as well as in cities in many foreign countries.

It is not the giver's responsibility to co-opt the vision of an organization but to help accomplish it.

A spiritual example of such growth is again the *Jesus* film teams of Campus Crusade. These thousands of teams show the *Jesus* film several times a week in cities and villages worldwide in even more settings than McDonald's. Not only do these teams successfully adapt to almost every culture and condition in the world, they can be made up of people of all ages. With a relatively small amount of training, college students to senior citizens can effectively use this medium. This kind of ministry can grow, which makes it a good investment.

Growth also relates to the internal organizational integrity of the ministry making the appeal. Do they have the administrative people power and systems necessary to sustain growth? Are their projections accurate? Is it reasonable to expect them to fulfill their goals? All these factors affect growth.

Finally, growth looks at the historical timing or potential of the ministry. Are they in an opportunity that has diminished, or is the opportunity increasing? For example, we stopped supporting a military ministry when the air force base it served closed. This ministry had been effective, but obviously with the closing, there was no future growth potential.

THEOLOGICAL EDUCATION

Beyond the opportunities developed with assistance from our MUSIG grid, one of the major spiritual ventures we support is theological education. This, of course, is where leadership for our churches and frontline organizations is developed. The understanding of biblical truth is so foundational to all that is attempted and accomplished.

Reportedly, more people are coming to Christ today than ever before—upward of 150,000 a day in the non-Western world alone! These numbers are astounding! The greatest need in the church today is for pastors and leaders for these new brothers and sisters in Christ. We support Dallas Theological Seminary, which has a great international program. Its foreign graduates go back home to their countries and minister to their own people, having had the best preparation possible. Many become the spiritual leaders of their countries.

An excellent worldwide organization, called Overseas Council for Theological Education, identifies and helps fifty-plus evangelical seminaries on six continents with over 14,000 students. But thousands more qualified students are waiting for scholarship help. Faculty help is needed. Buildings are needed. Otherwise we're moving these new believers in the front door of the church and, with little or no trained leadership, they will stumble out the back door! I believe this great need for international pastors/leaders should be the church's number one priority today. (See appendix 2 for information on how you can help Dallas Theological Seminary and Overseas Council.)

Larry Burkett, founder of Christian Financial Concepts, a Christian financial counseling organization, points out that an important function of a Christian's business should be to fund the proclamation of God's loving Word. The Bible says that we are to honor the Lord from the firstfruits of all our produce (Prov. 3:9). I take this seriously.

For those of us who have the ability to do so and the means to make it happen, we would be derelict in obedience to God's Word if we did any less than that. Surrendering our lives to Christ is the first step; surrendering our all—including our possessions—and prayerfully allowing His Holy Spirit to direct and control our lives completes what God asks. Not only are we to be hearers of the Word, but we must be doers also.

Ron Blue, another leader in Christian financial counseling, has a company that promotes seminars on incorporating solid biblical principles for good stewardship. Ron has a wonderfully wise suggestion, which I quote: "Do your givin' while you're livin' so you'll be a-knowin' where it's goin'!"

RIDING THE PIPELINE

15

At one point in my walk with God I had the feeling that I was missing some fulfillment. It was kind of like when part of your shoe—the heel—is worn off on one shoe more than the other. You can feel it; you notice it. What I was sensing was not something that I was necessarily overly troubled about, but it just seemed that there was something lacking.

About this time I went skiing in Colorado with some men from Search Ministry, an outreach ministry for adults. It was a gorgeous December day, clear blue sky, sunshine, plenty of snow, not too warm, not too cold—just a wonderful day for skiing.

The guys were all good athletes, aggressive, a push-it-to-the-limit kind of men, and we had these perfect conditions. There were no crowds. It couldn't have been better.

We were all blowing down the mountain, just flying. We'd ski down a ways, maybe sometimes even irresponsibly, then finally stop someplace, look at each other, and start laughing. We were actually giddy, having a "Rocky Mountain high." At some point that day I started asking myself a question: *Are thrills immoral and sinful?*

That question continued to play itself over and over in my head. What we were experiencing was so thrilling, so wonderful. Are thrills immoral and sinful?

After grappling with this question in my mind, I concluded

that our elation in thrilling moments is the way we were created . . . that thrills and enjoyment of this kind are not immoral. God made us this way and it is definitely, by itself, not sinful.

I thought about little kids loving Big Wheels; most babies enjoy being tossed in the air. We love slides, roller-coaster rides, bicycle riding, motorboating, and skimming across the water or snow. In all this kind of activity, there is a glee, a thrilling joy that comes.

You can't shoot the pipeline if you don't get out among the rocks and the big waves.

"Wow," I said to myself. "But this is just physical, and it's so thrilling. Then why isn't my spiritual life—my life in Christ—at least as thrilling, if not more so?"

I remember thinking about all of this and asking God about adventure. *I like adventure, God, and I don't want to leave anything on the table. I want to experience the fullness of John 10:10, "I came that they might have life, and might have it abundantly."*

Life to the full, that's what we want—the majestic, joyous fulfillment of God's creative intent for His children.

Riding the Oahu Pipeline

Several months later I was driving down the LBJ Freeway in Dallas and I was thinking again about this idea of adventure and thrills, and how, even though God was using me in my church and on ministry boards and even leading people to Christ and helping others grow through my efforts, something was missing. Then this thought came into my mind: *You can't shoot the pipeline if you don't get out among the rocks and the big waves.*

"What in the world am I thinking?" I wondered aloud. "I'm not even a surfer and here I was talking surfer language—rocks, waves, pipeline?"

I did some more thinking. The Pipeline is the name given to a well-known surfing spot on the north shore of Oahu, Hawaii. The waves are so large there that when they break they form a perfect curl or tube, making this the greatest surfing challenge in the world. The "curl" is the hollow of the wave, the sweet spot just inside the base of the wave's crest where surfers know they'll catch the perfect ride.

Most of us have seen footage of this on *Wide World of Sports*, where the wave curls around the surfer, propelling the surfboard and its rider forward. The ultimate for a surfer is to shoot the curl at Hawaii's Pipeline when the waves are up.

In his book *Beyond the Bottom Line*, Bill Lawrence describes it like this:

> From the shoreline the surfer, small and fragile, is dwarfed by the towering twenty-foot wave. He stands skillfully on his tiny board, totally unprotected, exposed to all the power of the water, taking some of the greatest forces of nature head-on. Engulfed by the spray of the wave, the surfer disappears, only to reappear out of the mist, still upright on his board, staying with it until the wave laps the shore. He has survived the greatest challenge and risk in surfing; he has ridden the Pipeline.[1]

I thought about how surfing could be an analogy for the Christian life. I imagined how I could start going to the gym to get "pumped up," sit under a sunlamp for a period of time and get myself a good tan, and then find an instructor and learn how to surf.

I could then actually go down to the beach, drag along all the right paraphernalia (the surfboard and necessary equipment), wear the right clothes (gym boxers), dye my hair, get a four-wheel-drive car, and maybe end up looking like some great old-timer surfer. But the bottom line is, if I stayed in the lagoon, playing in the waves and maybe even surfing a little bit, sure, I could call myself a surfer. You can do that as a Christian too. I could look just like a faithful, lay-it-on-the-line believer even though I really wasn't one.

The people who really get to experience the ultimate thrill of surfing are those who get out there where the big waves are—the Pipeline. They take the risk of riding those towering twenty-foot waves and being propelled toward the rocks, flying above the killer reefs below. These are the surfers who are layin' it on the line! Can—should—the Christian life be like that too?

Where's the Thrill?

I carried this surfing analogy over to personal ministry. I thought about how a person can go to church, be involved on boards, wear the right clothes, and say the right things, but if you don't go out there at risk and lay it on the line for God, you'll miss His best.

What came to mind was Hebrews 11:6, which says that without faith it is impossible to please God, that you must believe that He is God, and that He is a rewarder of those who seek Him.

My mind skipped to Galatians and those verses about the fruit of the Spirit being love, joy, peace, patience, kindness, goodness, faithfulness, gentleness, and self-control (Gal. 5:22-23). I tied all of these verses together in my thinking and came back again to what John 10:10 describes about life ("I came that they might have life, and might have it abundantly"). I felt I was on to something. In my thinking this must be the abundant life—"exceeding abundantly," beyond all you can ask or think! Faith and fruit! And it's only available through laying out your life for God in faith!

Another thing I thought about: The Scriptures also say that we are not to test God (Luke 4:12). So there's some point when you push God in faith where eventually you might get to the place where you are testing Him. You can actually go past faith into testing God, which is too far. The height of pleasing Him is quite possibly at the height of faith, just before you get to testing.

So I always come back to John 10:10 and the abundant life that He wants us to have. In summary, I believe that to please God in faith and to believe that He is a rewarder is to push out in faith to a point just short of testing God. Regular personal prayer and devotional times define this for me.

If you could draw a line that goes from low faith to medium faith to high faith, I want to live with the Spirit's leading right at the *top* of faith in God—just before I reach foolishness. It's where you step out in faith, like Abraham and all those other Old Testament heroes and heroines of the faith, and pray something like, "I don't have that perfect sense of clear direction, Lord, but I'm going to take this step of faith. Please guide me in Your way, and close the door if I'm wrong."

You've probably prayed something like that before. It goes back to the attitude and motive of the heart. If your intentions are to please God and further the kingdom, and it is a step of faith, He isn't going to let you down!

What an adventure life is when we leave room for God to do the exceeding abundant things above all that we can ask or think!

I wondered if I was thinking correctly—to want thrills in my spiritual life, thrills in Christ? I knew I wanted to obey God, to further His kingdom, and to bring praise, honor, and glory to His name.

I've now thought about this hundreds of times, and it all makes sense to me. It helps me to understand that it's okay to want to experience life more abundantly, to ask Him for exactly what He wants for me. This is not making demands; I'm just telling Him I don't want to fall short of anything He wants for me because I haven't asked and tried.

Please understand me, I'm not talking about material things; that's up to Him. I'm talking about my one-on-one life with Christ. I want to be a doer of the Word and not just a hearer (James 1:22). I want to be a part of the "greater works" Christ said we would do (John 14:12).

The Bible says we have not because we haven't asked, or we've asked amiss (James 4:3). I don't want to be a "have not."

As a result of thinking these thoughts, praying, and seeking His will, and fervently desiring to please Him, many things began happening to Anne and me, as well as to Interstate. The blessings and thrills of being a risk taker for God, putting His interests above all others and managing the business God's way—lovingly, boldly, and generously— keep me paddling out to the deep water to ride God's "Pipeline" every day.

Trusting and obeying God mean sometimes negotiating my way through high, treacherous, and surging walls of water, and I've fallen off the board a time or two. But it's so thrilling! My heart is happy today—far more happy than it ever was when I was just putting in hard work, long hours, and living on the low level of the natural, the ordinary, and the explainable.

What an adventure life is when we leave room for God to do the exceeding abundant things above all that we can ask or think!

TAPPING INTO THE POWER

16

I'm a battery guy—I should know all about power sources. But for the longest time I just didn't understand how to tap into the great source of power in the Christian life—prayer. Now I know better. I've learned where you have to go to tap into that direct current of spiritual power from God Himself.

I certainly agree with Dr. Bill Bright, founder and president of Campus Crusade International, who says that there is absolutely nothing more important in the believer's life than prayer. God has made available to us through prayer a vast reservoir of power, wisdom, and grace—if only we are willing to faithfully claim His promises.

Bill taught me the importance of 1 John 1:9—one of my all-time favorite verses, which is about prayerful confession and how to keep short sin accounts with God. That verse reads: "If we confess our sins, He is faithful and righteous to forgive us our sins and to cleanse us from all unrighteousness." That's been a *big* help to me because I sin often. So I try to confess my sins as I go and as God reveals them to me—not just at night, not at a specified prayer time in the morning, but *as soon* as I realize I'm off track with God. This keeps me clean before God, close to Him, and ready to serve Him.

Another Scripture related to prayer also had a major impact on me. James 5:16 reads, "The effective prayer of a righteous man can accomplish much." So I had to analyze myself to see if I was a righteous man. When I first read this verse, I began to look through the Bible for verses that told me how to be righteous. For whatever reason, I couldn't quite find what I was after. Instead I found 1 John 1:9, which explained how to get rid of all unrighteousness. So I determined, "Okay, then what's left must be righteous."

Well, that may not be how your mind works to figure something like that, but it made sense to me, and God has honored it in my life. So if it seems your prayers aren't being productive, you might want to consider looking at it like this also. Just remember, keep short accounts with God and confess your sins. I can assure you, God is "faithful and just" to keep His part of the deal, just like the Bible says.

GIVE THANKS

There's one other little thing I do that might be helpful to you. Once I was reading in Romans 1 about how even though men know God, they do not honor Him as God or give thanks (vv. 18-21). After seeing that, I bowed my head and said, "God, I may not do a lot of things that You want me to do, but I can say thank you. So I covenant with You that I'll always remember to say 'Thank You.'"

I use mealtimes to trigger my memory of that promise I made. Not only do I thank Him then for my food, but, more so, I thank Him for all He's done for me—it is simply a matter of honoring the commitment I made to Him. I seem to get hungry every four or five hours, so I thank Him on a pretty regular basis.

Pray *All* the Time

The Bible says to pray "without ceasing" (??????????). How do you do that? How can you pray without stopping when you are busy in the daily heat of it all—earning a living, raising a family, chasing all your activities, and just doing all the things of life?

I finally discovered that it's an attitude of prayer you can have on an ongoing basis during your waking hours, regardless of what you are doing or where you are. It's an inner dialogue with God, a communion of dependence and trust in thought with Him. It doesn't depend on posture or place—certainly, we all can't be on our knees in some secluded place praying all the time. We are to be doers of the Word too!

My feeling, however, is that every person does need to have some special, secluded, quiet, private time in the Bible and in prayer with God to really draw near to Him.

I've only learned the importance of this myself in the last few years. Before, I had often given God time on the run—literally. I like to jog, so I began to pray for people in the homes I passed while running. I knew many of them, so I'd mention their names. Then I thought, *Oh, I can do this also for all my family and other friends.* I would spend twenty to thirty minutes jogging and raising up people's names, asking God to help them draw closer to Him and to bless their families.

The problem was that my jogging was intermittent, and therefore my intercessory prayers were also not consistent. So I made a list of people and their prayer needs and prayed for them more regularly. But I still didn't have a specific quiet time.

I also used to pray whenever I had some slack time—in the car while driving or when stuck in a traffic jam or on an airplane—sort of praying as I went. I'd put stick-'ems on my mirror at home to remind me of requests, but I was getting more and more of them, and I couldn't remember them all. I knew I was forgetting some, and I was feeling guilty about it.

Evangelist Leighton Ford had taught me that when someone asks you to pray for them, do it right then—to be sure you do it. I did that some of the time, but I knew I needed to pray more regularly and more often for people. I was becoming overwhelmed with it all.

I'd wake up in the morning, and during my normal get-ready-to-go-to-work routine, I'd pray. I was trying to pray for a lot of people and situations, but I'd lose track and get distracted. There were many times I would start praying in the morning when I woke up and I wouldn't finish specific prayers until I'd put my head down at night to go to sleep. Have you ever done that? I'd rationalize and think, *Well, it's okay, you're praying continually,* but I knew something was missing.

I have always liked doing my serious thinking in the morning—in the shower and while shaving. In the process of waking up, facing the day, and thinking about what I'm going to be doing, my mind will freewheel. A lot of my creativity and direction has always come during these times. So this favorite time to ponder life and my desire to pray were in conflict.

Hard-Knock Education

As often seems to be the case, I needed a hard whack upside my head to change my ways. A major personal crisis rocked the foundation of my life and literally knocked me to my knees (which was new for me), and I began to pray desperately. During that time, God revealed some deep-seated sin in my life—hypocrisy, hard-heartedness, bitterness, and abusive language and manner. He let me see my behavior, like a motion picture, and it broke my heart. But it also drove me to the Scriptures, to deeper confession, and to dedicated prayer. In the midst of all this I realized that I had never given Him my prime time. It was like I was keeping Him on hold most of the time. The crisis forced a change.

One day I remembered how Christ had prayed early in the morning, usually before daylight. I know this probably sounds simplistic, but I decided that if this was good enough for Jesus, it was good enough for me!

I started an early morning quiet time, which was kind of hard for me because I had to give up *my* morning creative-thinking time. But the results were amazing. I built up a list of prayer requests and prayed through it every day. The list grew and grew, and I found that if I prayed this way, I had a wonderful, close time with God.

For the first year or so it was easy to do—I'd pop out of bed early, get situated, and go at it no matter how early it was (one morning I got up at 2:45 because I had an early flight). But as time has passed, it has become harder, requiring more self-discipline and commitment. I still struggle off and on with it, but the effort is so worthwhile. Often I spend long times on my knees in prayer, and God nourishes my heart and soul. I have seen many of my prayer requests come to pass as the days and years unfold.

Cranked Up Good for God

People have asked me, "Well, Norm, how do you pray? Do you have some kind of a format?"

When I begin praying for others, I start out raising up all the names on my list along with any situations which I know need specific prayer. Then I present all family members by name, even my extended family—brothers and their families, brothers-in-law and their families (our nieces and nephews), other relatives, our close friends and neighbors—the president, our government leaders and those in authority, ministries—Billy Graham, Bill Bright, Chuck Colson, Charles Stanley, Chuck Swindoll, Luis Palau, and on and on—and our church and its pastors and leaders, and I ask God to include their families. I ask Him to bless their loved ones, from the grandparents on down, so I try to cover two or more generations.

I pray for the prisoners I meet as we do prison outreach visitation, for every person involved in incarceration, and for all the prisons in the world. (I specifically say "every individual in the world who is locked up.") I intercede for Interstate Batteries' people—our leadership, all our other personnel and suppliers, our distributors and dealers, and their employees and families. Prayer is always made for our NASCAR racing team.

I appeal to God for every person in the world who doesn't know Him and His blessed Son, Jesus Christ. At first this seemed far-fetched to me, but God reinforced in my heart through the Scriptures that it's good and right to pray for the whole world and that He desires all to be saved and not one to perish.

I pray, too, that God will soften our hearts and convict us of all our sins. That He will give us hearts of confession and repentance. That He will help us draw near to Him and love Him more each instant.

That He will help us to be more faithful, obedient, loving, kind, humble, serving, generous, and filled with His Spirit. And that we would have the mind of Christ and be conformed to His image. I pray that, as His laborers, He will grant us the chance to independently and corporately bring forth much fruit for His kingdom and that our lives would fill Him with good pleasure and bring praise, honor, and glory to His Name.

Prayer *and* Fasting

In the summer of 1994 I was honored to be included with hundreds of other brothers and sisters in Christ at a meeting in Florida where, through fasting and prayer, we asked God to forgive and heal our nation. There was a great spiritual oneness, a unity among us, and a dependency on God's supernatural power—it was a coming together that honored God. It was wonderful!

Jesus spoke of fasting with praying, yet to my knowledge few do it, let alone encourage it. God tells us many times to do things, and there are great consequences that come from them. There are physical benefits that come from fasting, for sure, but this is definitely not the primary reason why we should fast and pray. Christ said it was a valuable weapon in the war we wage with the devil. So, if we're not fasting, we're depriving ourselves of a powerful weapon in our warfare. And by fasting, we are also showing God through sacrificial commitment that we are willing to humble ourselves before Him and to be vigilant as prayer warriors against the adversary.

So this priority for prayer has literally changed my life. And by the way, I still pray often when I'm jogging or on the go. But now it's an add-on, not my dedicated time to bow down and talk with my Father in heaven and tap into all that fantastic power just waiting to be used.

MOVE TO THE FRONT

17

H ave you ever thought that life should be more fulfilling and significant, that life should have more excitement and adventure?

Well, if you have, you're right! It should and it can! I want to share with you how it happened for Anne and me.

Several years ago we traveled to Romania when the "Iron Curtain" was still up. We wanted to see the results of some giving we had done in support of a ministry that had been forced to work in secret in that country. It was a wonderful experience in that we saw firsthand the fruit of our ministry assistance, and God gave us a special love for the Romanians.

However, something else welled up strong in our hearts—a desire not just to *see* ministry but to *do* ministry. We said if and when we ever took another trip like that, it would include a way to participate.

A couple of years later Anne did just that when she returned to communist Romania undercover for an eight-day ministry of teaching pastors' wives. (Don't miss chapter 18 for Anne's account of this experience.) Upon her return to the U.S., her spirit was overjoyed and her faith and enthusiasm were at an all-time high. This joy spilled over into all areas of her life, especially her personal ministry outreaches here at home.

Since then, we've been on several short-term mission trips where we actually participated. We have ministered on the front lines in Russia, Bulgaria, Albania, Estonia, Romania, Mongolia, and in Central and South America, as well as in U.S. prisons. Each experience rekindles that initial exuberance, that desire to be *doing* ministry. Neither Anne nor I will ever be content to just participate from a distance again. We need to be out on the front line some of the time, in addition to the normal, day-to-day call God has on our lives.

Joy Inexpressible

The apostle Peter speaks of rejoicing with "joy inexpressible" (1 Peter 1:8) and that's just how it feels when it comes to trying to describe what it's like to take the Word of God to people who've never heard it before. I still don't quite know what it is. I suspect that it has a lot to do with seeing the face of God in people different from ourselves as we love them with the love of Christ. All I know is that after having experienced it some, it's been such a lift to my spiritual walk and my closeness to God.

You've got to be willing to get out of yourself and lay your life and your means on the line for the Lord if you want to really experience the wonder of God.

Anne and I now have a ministry called Front Line Outreach that takes us to Mexico, overseas, and into U.S. prisons on a regular basis. And while we know that everyone can't do everything, we also know God enables the faithful to do great things beyond their dreams.

Everyone who is faithfully obedient to God's leading will experience the wonderful fullness of life that is God's most kind intention for His beloved children. So that's what this chapter is all about. Hopefully, our experiences will incite a desire in *your* heart to be on the front line wherever you are.

Laying Your Life on the Line for the Lord

Anne and I had often talked about why so many people seem "dead" in church pews. Why wasn't the Christian life more thrilling, joyful, adventuresome, dynamic? About this time I encountered the surfing analogy to the Christian life, and we both came to the conclusion that you've got to be willing to get out of yourself and lay your life and your means on the line for the Lord if you want to really experience the wonder of God.

In *My Utmost for His Highest,* Oswald Chambers talks about how faith must be a tremendously active principle and the need for a Christian to venture out *in faith.* Chambers wrote:

> God brings us into circumstances in order to educate our faith, because the nature of faith is to make its object real. . . . Faith is the whole man rightly related to God by the power of the Spirit of Jesus Christ.[1]

Another book I'd recommend you read to light your fire, "shake your salt," and help you shine light is Chuck Swindoll's *Simple Faith.*

Anne and I became convinced that we wanted others to experience what we were increasingly experiencing, so we invited our friends, relatives, and business associates to join us in some ministry adventures. I knew that these folk really *did* want their lives to count, but a lot of people can't afford the time or the money to be traipsing all over the place all the time. So we began to pray, asking God to show us what to do to get others motivated.

FLO: Front Line Outreach

It was Anne who came up with the name FLO—Front Line Outreach—in answer to people asking us, "How can we find out about these trips? How can we become involved?"

We sent a letter to our friends introducing them to this new ministry God had led us to start. We even came up with a mission statement for FLO: "The purpose of FLO is to help Christians draw closer to God through experiencing the wonderful fulfillment of being used by Him in hands-on, frontline evangelism and discipleship."

Right up front we explained that we weren't requesting funds but were presenting them with an opportunity to grow even closer to God while letting Him crank up their faith as He moved them to a higher level of personal fulfillment and adventure. Since then we've had some great times. But when you go to the front of God's battle lines, look out; the enemy will be using real bullets.

Satan's Territory

I have learned, not just in traveling to foreign countries but through going into prisons in this country, that evangelistic outreach means moving into Satan's territory. This is what I've come to grips with—that we go into areas where Christians, in some ways, have pretty much surrendered ground to evil. There is something different about going out into enemy territory as opposed to leading people to Christ primarily in one's own territory. But the spiritual rewards are awesome.

There is something there—in unfamiliar turf—that has the dynamic to turbocharge your faith. It *really* has ratcheted up my faith. There is a godly payoff, if I can put it in a businessperson's terms. But of greater significance is the fact that the unsaved and the hurting need us and God blesses us for going.

Our nation's prisons certainly represent one of those places where evil is pervasive. I think of a lockdown cell block in Caldonia, North Carolina, where I sat in front of a little six-inch-by-twenty-inch square piece of Plexiglas to communicate with a prisoner. A guard had approached me earlier and said, "This guy over here wants to ask you a question about NASCAR racing."

The opening in the steel door was so small, I could only see the guy's mouth moving and his eyes and that was about it. So he yelled to me a question about Ernie Irvin, a NASCAR driver who had gotten hurt.

After some small talk and answering the prisoner's question, I started asking him about his spiritual bent. I could tell he was beating around the bush, and his eyes were looking over my shoulder. He was being polite, but he wasn't with me; he wasn't interested in the way the conversation was going.

Then he said, "Can you excuse me a minute? I have to make a call." He walked to the back of the cell and started yelling through the concrete. When he came back, he said, "Excuse me, but the exercise yard is behind my cell, and I had to tell my buddy something because he's only out there for a few more minutes."

There is something there—in unfamiliar turf—that has the dynamic to turbocharge your faith.

We resumed the conversation and again he wasn't being responsive, although he was polite. He apologized and said, "We're supposed to go outside, and these other guys in my block are waiting." (By this time the guard had opened a small food tray slot in the door so we could talk better.)

I said, "Use your mirror." I knew that when he put his little four-inch mirror out of the opening he could look to the right and to the left out of his cell. He was antsy and nervous, but after looking with his mirror, he could see that some other inmates were also in conversation with other counselors.

I continued, "Let me ask you something. If you could double the enjoyment in your life right now, would you do it?"

"Yeah!" he responded.

"Then let me take you through this little booklet," I said. "This information is capable of getting you to where you can double or triple your enjoyment in life right here in this prison."

The inmate pulled up a trash can, tipped it upside down, and sat down. I took him through *The Four Spiritual Laws* (appendix 3), and I could tell from the first law, which speaks about God's love for us and the wonderful plan He has for our lives, that his face was changing. Now his eyes were focused, and he was reading ahead of me.

The first law asks why everybody isn't experiencing that wonderful plan, and the answer is man's sin. "We have all sinned against God and gone our own way." Now there was a much different look in the prisoner's eyes, the Holy Spirit had turned the lights on.

We continued and eventually he prayed to receive Christ. I was showing him more when the guard came and said we had to go. The inmate said to the guard, "All I wanted to do was ask him about Ernie Irvin, and he got me, he got me!" But there was a happy note sounding in his voice. I hadn't got him. *God* had got him!

Anne and I participate on a regular basis in similar prison visitations with Bill Glass Ministries, a national prison ministry to those incarcerated. We experience the joy of sowing and reaping the harvest, along with other counselors and individuals from across the U.S. who have responded to Jesus' words: "I was in prison, and you came to Me. . . . To the extent that you did it to one of these brothers of Mine, even the least of them, you did it to Me" (Matt. 25:36, 40).

What I try to do after such visits is to put the names of these men on my prayer list. We can't always send books or write letters, but we are able to take in discipleship booklets and sign the prisoners up for a Bible study.

During these spirit-charged weekend visits, we hear stories that are very sad, particularly those of young people. One fourteen-year-old boy told how he was in for murder and had killed for the first time at the age of nine following an armed robbery. A young thirteen-year-old girl spoke of the multiple sexual encounters she had already experienced. We hear stories of money, cars, drugs, gangs, power, jewelry—all the trappings of the world not satisfying the search of these inmates. This search for something that would take them higher and give meaning to their lives is often what led to their present condition and incarceration.

But on the flip side of the sad stories is how God works in giving prisoners an eternally happy ending as a result of hearing the gospel and responding.

Front Line Outreach provides some scholarship assistance for those who want to participate in prison outreaches. The groups with whom we work in enemy territory need workers. Scripture says that we should pray that the Lord of the harvest will raise up laborers who will go forth into His harvest (Matt. 9:38).

God owns the harvest that is produced by distress and conviction of sin, and this is the harvest we have to pray that laborers will be thrust out to reap. People all around us are looking for life's answer and are therefore "ripe to harvest." Our hearts have been changed forever by our experiences in prison ministries. God is *so* good—especially in the middle of enemy territory!

TO RUSSIA WITH GOD'S LOVE

Anne and I flew to Russia in 1990 with Dr. Bill Bright and Paul Eschelman as a part of the Campus Crusade entourage when the *Jesus* film premiered. Imagine the thrill of taking the life of Christ from the book of Luke, in living color and in the Russian language, for the first time to the people of Russia! What an incredible adventure and privilege!

The premiere of the *Jesus* film was a "By Invitation Only" event for the entertainment avant-garde of Moscow. One of the things that was so great about it was that on that very same night Ted Turner and Jane Fonda premiered the Russian version of *Gone with the Wind*. We outdrew *Gone with the Wind* with the life of Christ!

More than eighteen hundred members of the Russian Academy of Arts and Sciences were present at the *Jesus* film premiere. This group is the equivalent of our country's Screen Actors Guild. We had hundreds of requests for invitations, and the film had to be shown in two different theaters that night, then repeated again on a Saturday night. So it was double what we had anticipated, with more than 3,500 people seeing the *Jesus* film (over half of the academy's membership!).

Eight of the eleven ministers of Russia were at that premiere in Moscow. Later, I met the deputy minister of education and asked her what she thought of the film. She said, "I think that film should be seen in all the Russian schools."

Little did I know that God would bring together the largest consortium of Christian ministries ever (The CoMission—over seventy ministries; appendix 2) to team up with the Russian government to train Russian schoolteachers in curriculum for teaching the truth of Christ to their students. As of March 1996, 35,700 teachers had completed this training, which includes the *Jesus* film as part of the curriculum. Over 17,000 of these teachers prayed to receive Christ during their training, and surveys have established that 27,489 are teaching the curriculum in their schools, with 32,130 saying they've shown the film, which includes a salvation invitation to their students, What a miracle!

We outdrew *Gone with the Wind* with the life of Christ!

Another day, in the Kremlin, we gave out The Four Spiritual Laws, Josh McDowell's More Than a Carpenter (in Russian), and Russian New Testaments. It was unforgettable. There was a subway exit just across the street from the Kremlin, and when people would get off their trains I would hand them The Four Spiritual Laws in Russian. As these folks stepped up to the stoplight, they'd start reading. Instead of walking across when the light changed, many of them would stand there reading through several changes of the light. Then they'd turn around and come back, with tears in their eyes, and ask if they could have more copies.

As I was giving out illustrated New Testaments in Red Square, I saw lots of schoolchildren with their teachers, and it dawned on me that I should give those Bibles to the teachers. I started doing this and then watched as the kids swarmed around the teachers. The kids wanted to be read the New Testament right there in Red Square where the high-stepping, uniformed guards were marching.

Fun for Jesus

Following our stay in Moscow, we headed to Leningrad but got delayed in the airport for eight hours. Everything was backed up and there were people wall-to-wall. So we began to pass out *The Four Spiritual Laws* throughout the airport. It was a fun thing to do. After about an hour you couldn't find anybody in that airport who wasn't reading or talking about those little booklets.

I never will forget this one scarf-clad babushka, standing with her mop in a bucket of water, leaning up against the wall with one leg crossed over the other while she read the booklet. I thought as I watched her, *We've pretty well covered the territory—from the high officials in government to the men and women on the street to teachers and schoolchildren to international travelers to this vintage Russian woman. What an adventure, Lord! This is so exciting.*

Then I spied an empty table and a chair, and I began to lay *The Four Spiritual Laws* out across the table. Whenever someone would walk by and look me in the eye, I would just look them right back and wave my hand across the table, nodding and saying "Free!" They would pick them up eagerly and go off and read them. Often they'd return with tears in their eyes. One guy came back with a whole soccer team, wanting to know if they could each have one. It was unbelievable. It was a confirmation to me from God that He'd heard my prayers as I had cried out longing for my Christian walk to be more thrilling and more meaningful.

Finally we boarded the plane for Leningrad and found ourselves sitting on the tarmac for another two hours. But it wasn't wasted time. The late Colonel Glenn Jones was part of the Campus Crusade group, and he was sitting next to this guy in uniform who had the window seat. Glenn looked at him, reached across, and gave him one of *The Four Spiritual Laws*.

The man spoke to Glenn in German. Glenn told him he didn't speak German, and the man said, "Oh, you speak English," and they conversed. After giving him the booklet, Glenn said, "This is very important to your life," and the man said, "Okay, I'll read it."

Glenn found the rest of us on the plane and asked us to pray for the man. Thirty minutes later, after thoroughly reading the booklet cover to cover, the man pulled something from his wallet and showed it to Glenn. It was a cross. The man told Glenn he was also a colonel, and that years ago he'd received the cross and had kept it hidden away. But now he had a desire to know the truth about God.

Glenn asked him if he'd prayed the prayer printed in the booklet, and the German colonel said yes, that he knew he needed God. He asked Glenn if he had any more of *The Four Spiritual Laws*, and could he get a hundred or so? He wanted to give them to all his men.

On that flight to Leningrad my seatmate was a young girl, and I gave her a copy of that little booklet. She'd read a little of it, and then she'd put it down and take a tissue and dab at her eyes. Then she'd read some more and cry again. And that's the way it went until she finished. Finally, she folded the pamphlet up and gave it back to me. I motioned, "No, it's for you." So she took it back, put it in her purse, then took my hand and thanked me.

I looked at her and said, "Do you speak English?" and she said she didn't. So I pointed to a copy of the booklet, then I opened it up to the prayer, pointed to it and to her heart, and said, "You," and then pointed to heaven and to her heart. She, too, pointed to heaven and put the booklet to her heart, nodded, and smiled. I knew she'd invited Christ into her heart.

Once in Leningrad we used the same approach to show the *Jesus* film that we had in Moscow. This time I went behind the screen so I could watch the faces of those about to view the film. In the audience I saw several high Russian Orthodox priests, including the priest for the whole region, an old man with flowing white hair. Also, the mayor of Leningrad, the third most popular guy in Russia at the time, was there with his wife and two children. Everyone heard and saw the gospel in living color for the first time. It was thrilling!

These previews and the receptions that followed were big happenings with special singing, music, and celebration. Just how big and important we may not have fully realized at the time.

Sharing the Good News on Another Continent

Only five days after leaving Leningrad, on another continent and in a totally different culture, I experienced exactly the same wonderful sensation of seeing God change lives. As I stood in a rocky, muddy street in Venezuela, God made me aware of what was taking place. It was like He communicated, "Norm, I've just allowed you to be a part of My salvation for deprived, needy, and hurting people in one continent, and now here again with these people in Venezuela."

There is a universality of need and, for me, it was a confirmation of Scripture that God's Word is for all nations, tribes, and people (John 3:16-17), that the faithful proclamation of His Word will not return void (Isa. 55:11), and that the Word brings forth conviction of sin and our need to get right with God (John 16:8).

Hands-On Ministry

Some of the trips we've taken with groups have been as short as three days, others as long as two weeks or more.

In 1993 we traveled to the once Russian-occupied Baltic Sea nation of Estonia, to the half-million-populated capital city of Tallinn. In the Old Town part of this ancient city, we felt like we were back in thirteenth-century Europe, walking on cobblestone streets that were laid seven hundred years ago.

Everyone heard and saw the gospel in living color for the first time. It was thrilling!

Our goal in Tallinn was to work with our teammates, Global Mission Fellowship (GMF), to assist the nationals (members of the local churches—mostly young people—who spoke English) in planting new churches. It was hands-on mission involvement that some in our group of thirty-two people had never experienced before. No training was necessary; everything was provided for our team.

The areas we visited were targeted by mother churches in Tallinn, with translators, materials, and follow-up. We worked with Christian nationals and went door-to-door presenting the message of Christ.

The week's intense efforts were blessed by God. The results of our sharing included 262 professions of faith, churches either started or cranked up, and countless seeds planted for God and the Estonian Christians to grow and harvest.

Another wonderful outgrowth of these efforts was the teaching and training of the nationals in evangelism. It was a blessing to see the progress of our new friends as they experienced what God can do when they boldly share their faith.

One of our groups later told us that their translator was very reluctant to go door-to-door. In a loving yet persistent way, they encouraged him to participate. The first person he witnessed to accepted Christ. After that experience, the translator would almost run to the next door to share his faith.

Up to this point, the Estonian Christians' knowledge and participation in evangelism had been limited. This was due largely to the fact that until 1991 they had not been able to share their faith openly without fear of reprisal from the Communists.

Each night we were part of an open-air evangelistic preaching service. Not only did we have opportunities to lead people in a foreign country to a new life in Christ, but there was the added joy of knowing that our witness helped build up churches in a country where churches had long been oppressed.

Once again in Estonia we saw firsthand how God's Spirit moves as He changes lives on the front line and brings hope to those who once had little or no hope.

Dispelling Darkness

Charles Swindoll says that "Ours is a hell-bound, degenerate world," a world that is a "war zone full of foes that must be faced," and the only strategy that works in the real world and makes a lasting impact is by shaking salt and shining light (Matt. 5:13-16).[2] What is the purpose of salt? It preserves. It arrests corruption. What is the purpose of light? Light dispels darkness.

In pointing out these simple truths, Swindoll says too many

Christians are just shining their lights on each other. Jesus says to shine for the world—to shine our lights into the darkness, where it is really needed. "Spend less time in your own well-lighted all-Christian world and more time in the darkness."[3]

Seeking to dispel darkness is what Front Line Outreach is all about. As we sought more ways whereby we could be on the front line we were presented with an opportunity to team up with the staff of Campus Crusade and share the good news with the people of Monterrey, Mexico. It was an exceptional trip.

South of the Border

Monterrey is a city of 3.2 million people, surrounded on all sides by beautiful mountains. We traveled to a local neighborhood where the *Jesus* film had already been shown. We split into groups of three to four (each group included two or three nationals) and went door-to-door, witnessing in the mud street barrios to those who had and had not seen the film. We also passed out tracts in the marketplace and traveled into the neighborhoods of Vitro and San Bernabe to show the film. Before each showing our teams walked with translators through these neighborhoods, sharing our faith and passing out flyers with information about the upcoming film.

The film was shown in an interesting setting. There was a big mountain between us and the city lights of Monterrey, and the screen was set up with the mountain serving as a backdrop. The mountain outline was illuminated with a halo of light coming from behind it where the city lights were so bright.

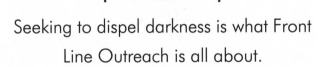

Seeking to dispel darkness is what Front
Line Outreach is all about.

An unusual thing happened. A big transformer in the distance blew up like a bomb when it was hit by a bus. There was an enormous explosion and the lights went out in all the surrounding barrios. Now there were no running jukeboxes in bars, no TVs in houses, no power *period.* Since we use a generator to run the film projector, we had the only juice in the area! In the darkness the only "game" in that barrio was the life of Christ in our movie!

Over twelve hundred people gathered in a large open area to see the film, and hundreds remained afterward to find out more about this man called Jesus. Many prayed to receive Christ that night.

We spent the next day, Sunday, in the city visiting in different churches with the staff of Campus Crusade before returning to the neighborhoods where the film had been shown the night before. In the Vitro community scores of children heard the gospel in their own language with the help of a puppet named Omar. Some of the group participated in playing soccer with two teams of teenage boys, and afterward the boys listened as the gospel was shared with them. Ten of the boys invited Christ into their hearts.

We visited the University of Monterrey (the MIT of Mexico) and passed out tracts, shared the gospel, and reaped God's harvest.

God's Truth Is for Everyone

It is amazing to see how God has prepared hearts for our arrival and to see people so receptive to the gospel when we make trips to other countries. We thank God for those who accept Christ, for those who make recommitments, and for the many seeds that are planted and watered for a later harvest.

The more I share Christ in different situations—from coworkers to down-and-out problem prisoners, to political leaders in Eastern Europe—I see the universality of the truth of God.

Front Line Outreach has become a confirmation from God that He heard my cry that day on the mountainside in Colorado. This is *the* consummate adventure of a lifetime—to be part of what God is accomplishing in our generation. I pray that this chapter has poured a little gas on *your* fire to want to go to your front line with Christ and experience the fullness of life just as God has intended for us.

A RIDE WITH AN ANGEL

18

Angels are real popular these days. But I gotta tell you, I've believed in angels for a long time. No, I don't see angels hiding behind every telephone pole, but I *do* believe God sends these guardians and guides to further the spreading of the gospel, help us individually, and grow the church, even though I don't think we always recognize them when we see them.

I've learned about angels from Billy Graham's book *Angels,* and I've also learned about them from the experiences of my wife, Anne. And I don't think I'll argue with either one of them!

Anne met an angel in the disguise of a young woman in communist Romania in 1986. As you might guess, Anne calls her trip behind the Iron Curtain (without the authorities knowing who or why she was there) one of the most incredible experiences she's ever had. Her story of the young woman angel fills me with awe and humility every time I think about it. But before we share that story, let's let Anne explain how she ended up in Romania in the first place.

After Norm and I went to Europe in 1984 and learned firsthand about the work of Biblical Education by Extension (BEE), I couldn't get it out of my mind. I began praying in earnest about the work they were doing. I had told them that if they ever got anything started for women, I wanted to be one of the first to do it.

When the opportunity to go on this mission was actually presented to me, I jumped on it. Norm was behind me all the way.

You knew I would be, now didn't you? Even though the Communist regime was still in total control at this time, Anne and her BEE partner, Sherry, teamed up in Vienna and headed out to Romania. They stayed two nights in the home of a pastor in a town close to the Black Sea. She told me that this first town had terrible economic conditions. She and Sherry ate sparingly, wondering if they were literally taking food from the mouths of their hosts.

They start their day standing in breadlines at about 5:30 A.M., arrive at work at seven, get off at four, do their motherly/wifely chores, and go to bed.

"For every meal except one," Anne related to me, "we were served the same thing. Four adults and two children ate from a dish the size of a salad plate. It was lined with fatty summer sausage and goat cheese, and held tomatoes and cucumbers in the middle. We always had bread, but hesitated to butter it because we knew their ration for the month was only two pounds. We never left the table satisfied, and we never saw any fruit. And it was always the same vegetables—tomatoes and cucumbers."

I was amazed when Anne told me of her hosts' embarrassment with the inconsistent water supply and their inability to offer their guests even a cup of coffee because it was so expensive. Coffee sold on the black market for forty dollars a pound and was used as an incentive to get a doctor to come see a sick child or for some other emergency. Anne left most of the supplies that she had brought right there in that town.

"The pastor felt it was less risky for us to stay cloistered," said Anne. "So for two days we stayed in the house with the curtains drawn rather than be seen coming and going several times."

Every evening from five until nine the women held their meetings. All women work in Romania. They start their day standing in breadlines at about 5:30 A.M., arrive at work at seven, get off at four, do their motherly/wifely chores, and go to bed.

"But they welcomed the time they spent with us," reported Anne. "What joy it was to see how eager they were to learn! We taught through translators, which was very tedious. Sometimes the translation was good, but other times we spent the next evening straightening out things we found were mistranslated the night before. But the advantage of working through a translator was that it gave the women listening time to write. And write they did—every word!"

I think Anne's life was changing as much as the hearts of these overworked women. They had never been to a women's retreat, Bible study, or any activity even vaguely resembling the spiritual-growth opportunities available for women in America. They were able to attend a three-hour church service on Sundays, and many of the pastors were great, spiritual teachers.

"But as to the practical biblical teachings regarding child rearing or building relationships," Anne told me, "the women didn't have a clue. That's why the teaching BEE provided was so great."

Her face changed when she told me, "We always closed our meetings not with 'sentence' prayers but with 'paragraph' prayers. I've never heard such fervent prayers. They thanked us profusely for coming and asked us to tell the West not to forget them.

"We felt such a bond with these women and held hands and sang in our own languages 'Blest Be the Tie That Binds.'"

Anne's trip into Romania with Sherry was certainly dangerous, but these are faithful ladies. "The truth is," Anne says, "that the consequences for the nationals, the Romanians with whom I was ministering, were far more dangerous than the consequences for myself and Sherry. They were the ones in real danger because everything we were doing was against the law for Romanians. If we'd been caught, I doubt if the authorities would have done much more than question us, tear up our visas, and order us out of the country. The Christian citizens of Romania would have had to remain and face the wrath of the Secret Police."

Anne told me that if any of the Romanians had been caught hosting her and Sherry for a night they could have been fined a month's wages or worse because they had not requested permission to have foreigners in their homes.

It was also against the law for the Romanians to meet in a home for any religious teaching or for more than five people to assemble in a home for any purpose without a permit. It was even unlawful for them to converse with Westerners unless they reported the content of the conversation to the Secret Police. Moreover, it was unlawful for Romanians to have any printed material of a religious nature other than that approved by the state. Anne said they saw a lot of hand-copied materials as a result.

We never saw the young woman again. That train carrying our angel disappeared down the track, leaving us alone again in a strange city.

And even that little fact brought me up short. I can walk into a Christian bookstore and find books on everything it seems, from Chuck Colson to chicken wings, but these people were secretly hand copying biblical teaching materials so they and others could continue to grow in the faith and remain obedient.

Pondering that kind of dedication and hunger for the truth brought me to my knees in humility!

Anne and Sherry usually traveled every other day, early, by train. They tried to be inconspicuous, wearing no makeup or jewelry, dressing plainly and walking with their heads down to avoid making eye contact. Such was the joylessness of public life in Romania that this is how they needed to act in order to blend in with the other citizens. If stopped, they were prepared to say they were tourists. But one particular day they planned to journey to a city where it made no sense for tourists to visit, so they traveled on the train as though they were Romanians, planning on not speaking a word to anyone.

It was on this day the Lord sent a guardian angel to help them through the trip.

Riding with an Angel

The morning of their miraculous trip, the travel alarm did not go off. But why should I get in the middle of this story? Anne lived this adventure. I'll let her tell it!

We woke up, tried not to panic when we saw how late we were, and just started throwing things in the suitcase. We had washed our hair the night before but didn't have time to do anything with it so our hair stuck out all over!

We jumped on that train at 5:30 A.M., thinking, *Well, maybe we can get a compartment by ourselves and that will help us regain some composure and get organized.* We walked through the cars, hoping and praying that we would find an empty compartment so we wouldn't have to be so careful as we munched on our granola bars and orange juice, our "luxurious" Western breakfasts.

But it wasn't meant to be. We found a compartment and took our seats, holding our overnight bags with our food and one night's gear, having stored our big bags in lockers in Bucharest. Before we could sigh with relief, four more people piled into the compartment. That meant no talking, no reading, no eating (our food would give us away as foreigners).

Two hours into the journey the train stopped at a station. Several conductors boarded and began yelling out the name of the stop. Sherry was in charge of our travel arrangements and knew every stop the train was supposed to make. She saw me looking at her and simply shook her head. We sat.

A few minutes later the conductor did the same thing, yelling out the name of the town. A young woman sitting across from me had been asleep. Suddenly she woke with a start and questioned the conductor about the name of the stop. "Yes," he said.

The girl stood up, gave us a nod, took her stuff, and got off. I shot Sherry a panicky look, at which time she slowly got up, got her bag, and walked out. Soon after, I did the same. Somehow, inexplicably, we knew we were to follow that girl!

We stood with a crowd on the platform of the station for five to ten minutes. Another train pulled up. The young woman looked at us and said one word in English: "Accident." She got on the train; we got on.

Nobody else had stared at us as if they knew we were Americans. We felt like we blended in very well. So we couldn't figure out why this girl had picked us out, especially when we hadn't even uttered a word in English.

No backing out by this point! We figured that if we had been operating within the down-to-earth, practical, "natural" realm, we would have had every reason to feel uneasy and unsure of ourselves. Sherry had counted the stops of the other train, but we had not been able to see the names of the stations until we'd passed them. The next train our little angel led us to was a train making the milk run and stopping everywhere. And I do mean *everywhere.*

After three hours of traveling, the girl looked over at Sherry, caught her eye and nodded. The train pulled to the stop where we saw the name of our town on the sign above the platform. Off we climbed. We never saw the young woman again. That train carrying our angel disappeared down the track, leaving us alone again in a strange city. We walked into the train station, both marveling at what had transpired and wondering what would happen next. With God there's always another surprise right around the corner. Plan A had been for us to have been met by someone, but we were several hours late. Plan B was for us to stay in the waiting area with a train schedule under one arm. Our password was the Romanian word for peace.

Plan C was for us to walk out of the station and turn right. We followed Plan C and started walking. But there were several exit doors. Which door were we to use? We were each praying for a miracle of guidance.

I had prayed for three years to be able to take this trip to secretly teach Christian principles to believers in Romania, and I felt secure in the way we were walking as we left that train station. We had hoped to hail a taxi, but there were none. So we kept walking. After about a block Sherry said, "What do you think?" and I replied, "It feels right to me, let's keep going."

Would you believe that in that remote city of over one hundred thousand people in the far-off land of Romania, we walked right up to the entrance of the church that was expecting us? We had made two turns and just kept walking, fully confident that John 10:4 means what it says: "When he puts forth all his own, he goes before them, and the sheep follow him because they know his voice."

I felt a shiver go up my spine as Anne related this to me. It seemed further proof that God was surely guiding their every footstep through a mission in a land filled with lies and deceit, danger and spiritual darkness.

When Communism began to take root in Eastern Europe, the tightening of religious freedom also had begun. At first people gave in to it because of fear. Before long, whole countries like Romania began to become run down and everything was in short supply, including food. There was no incentive under the Communist system for anyone to better themselves. Everything was owned by the government and people lost the personal pride of ownership. I don't mean the pride of having more than others and feeling that makes one better than them. I mean the pride such as a farmer feels working his fields, or a small businessman seeing the fruits of his labors.

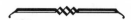

It's not only in places like Romania that the forces of darkness are working. It's all around us.

The communal system does not work without Christ as the center because it graduates to selfishness instead of love. And under that way of thinking, people simply stop caring.

But I learned from Anne the specifics of how God had not abandoned the believers in Romania. A group of pastors got together and decided that their purpose on this earth quite possibly included being martyred for Christ. And do you know what the reaction to such faith was? More fear? Not on your life! Fear left. Boldness took its place. Revival began.

The government responded to this lack of fear by trying a new strategy—taking over the seminaries to choke off the source of future Christian leaders. Their restrictions on the number of students entering one denomination's seminary allowed for only five graduates every four years to serve the needs of over a thousand churches that shared only 160 pastors!

God certainly blessed the teaching of Anne and Sherry to women in the underground church in Romania. She stood up to the powers of evil and darkness and confessed Jesus Christ as Lord in communist Romania. I'm awfully proud of her.

But it's not only in places like Romania that the forces of darkness are working. It's all around us. My ongoing prayer is that we who call ourselves Christians will always be found faithful to the call God has upon our lives.

I now know that we American Christians have an obligation to our brothers and sisters around the world to learn all that we can about their sufferings. How else can we help them and pray intelligently for them?

Jesus says in Luke, "From everyone who has been given much shall much be required" (12:48). What a privilege! What a joy!

A LIFE BEYOND THE NORM

19

Have you ever . . .

. . . sat in a race car, your whole body vibrating with the horsepower waiting to be unleashed by the touch of your hands and feet?

. . . hurt the person you loved the most in the whole world, and then turned around and done it again?

. . . said "why not?" and taken a chance, gone after a dream, shot a great wave in the Oahu Pipeline?

. . . risked everything to be obedient to God?

. . . asked for help, acknowledging that you are helpless over a certain area in your life?

. . . refused to help someone, then lived with the regret for the rest of your life?

. . . counted your abundant blessings and asked, "Why me?"

. . . totally lost it in anger and been too ashamed (or too proud) to ask for forgiveness?

. . . felt a hole in your heart so big that it swallowed your life?

. . . been cornered by your pride?

. . . been cornered by the Cross?

. . . watched your children pulling away, making their own mistakes, some of which look awfully familiar to you?

. . . cried over a beautiful sunset, a beautiful hymn, the beautiful feeling that your Father in heaven is preparing a home for you?

See, even crusty old Texans have a soft side.

I've experienced these and much, much more. Lately I've been thinking about what I have been, what I am now, and where I am going. Putting it into this book has been of great help in giving me the opportunity to do some more listening to the Spirit of God in my life. I've been surprised at some of the things I had forgotten (and probably should have forgotten) and at some of the things that have reminded me of how God has continually led me along His way. I've remembered friends from long ago and faced each new day with my dear Anne. I hope it doesn't take the writing of another book to remind me of all God's goodness all over again.

There were tough times to overcome in the early years, and I made some big-time mistakes.

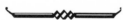

My memories of that great win at the Daytona 500 got me to thinking about Paul's images in his letters about racing. In 1 Corinthians 9:24 he wrote, "Do you not know that those who run in a race all run, but only one receives the prize? Run in such a way that you may win." Then in Philippians 3:14 he says, "I press on toward the goal for the prize of the upward call of God in Christ Jesus."

I can identify with those images, not only because of Interstate's racing teams, but because of my own life. A winning NASCAR Winston Cup racing team is a combination of a good car, good people, good fortune, courage, speed, fast decision making on your feet, adventure, cheering crowds, celebrities, fame, lots of money, and a straight-ahead approach without any distractions, giving it everything you've got.

What's at the end? A checkered flag, a trophy, a prize check, and then on to the next race. You might say that the *first* part of my life was that kind of a race: fast, hard, straightforward, going after what I wanted, blinders on so that I only focused on winning.

As you've read, though, that's not always how it turned out. Yes, I did learn, usually after a lot of trial and error. There were tough times to overcome in the early years, and I made some big-time mistakes. I knew how to party, how to drink a lot, and even how to set up my own illegal business during my college days. I often felt like that little boy getting up early to catch the bus to "The Pleasure Pier" in Galveston, dreaming about catching the mighty tarpon but not really having the right kind of bait and equipment. And in my first thirty-five years, I didn't have the right equipment for life either. I searched and searched for my place, my future, my purpose.

I married a most beautiful girl and then nearly blew it all due to alcoholism and ignoring her needs, not knowing how to be a godly leader in my own home. I went full speed ahead into Interstate Battery System and experienced phenomenal growth while I had a family at home who wondered who I was.

Then I met Jesus Christ and had my life turned upside down. He changed everything about that wild race. Now that I trust in Him more than anything, the business reflects His presence and my personal life depends on it.

But it is a verse in Ecclesiastes that says well the most important change in my life. It goes like this: "A cord of three strands is not quickly torn apart" (4:12). Those three strands represent God, Anne, and me. And as Anne and I have tried·to get closer to God, individually and also together, it has happened just as God promises in the "Good Book."

As I've said earlier, the adventurous and faith-building path God is leading us down keeps moving us more and more into the hands-on work of spreading the good news of Jesus Christ.

In January of 1991 we went to Outer Mongolia with three women and ten men upon the invitation of the government of that country. It was a three-day journey by air just to get there! The last leg we flew in an old bucket-of-bolts Russian Aeroflot plane that had long seen better days.

We were told that it would be at least twenty degrees below zero, so our carry-on bags were stuffed with layers of extra clothing. We definitely needed them when we landed—it was minus twenty-four degrees!

We learned that when the great explorer Marco Polo arrived in Mongolia he was told the people were ready to accept Christianity and that he should go back to Europe and return with missionaries. The story goes that when he went back he couldn't convince anyone to return to Mongolia with him.

As we entered frozen Mongolia, I found myself wondering, *What would have happened in this country if Christianity had grown instead of Buddhism?* I also wondered if I would have had the guts to go back to Mongolia with Marco Polo.

Mongolia is a tough, barren land, and in January in subzero temperatures, it was even more desolate than I ever imagined. The life expectancy there is barely over fifty years, and even today it is not unusual to find adults who bathe only a few times per year! (Of course, who could blame them when it's so cold?)

Many of the people on the outskirts of town still live in the traditional *ger*, the round Nomadic home of the Mongols that has a stove in the middle and its outer walls lined with animal skins. And, as you might have guessed, no indoor plumbing!

Our main reason for going was to show the *Jesus* film, which was dubbed into their Mongolian language. It was the first Western film ever presented in their tongue. I thought it was ironic that the film was shown in the Communist Cultural Center, right next door to the Stalin Museum, which had been closed. It was a pointed lesson to all of us about what really lasts in this world.

As the film was showing, I walked to the front of the auditorium and looked out at the people. It overwhelmed me that they were seeing the life of Jesus for the first time. I could literally see their faces changing as the story unfolded.

One of the national leaders who emceed for the night thanked us from the stage, saying, "Tonight you have shown the people of Mongolia how we can truly have our sins forgiven."

As we entered frozen Mongolia, I found myself wondering, *What would have happened in this country if Christianity had grown instead of Buddhism?*

One of the translators later said to us privately, "You mean there is a chance that this could be true, that there is another way for eternal life?" Later that weekend she prayed to receive Christ. There's no greater thrill than being a part of someone choosing God's gift of eternal salvation and His ongoing help for the here and now on this earth.

On another trip during an evangelistic crusade, I was sitting in a Russian soccer stadium near the Volga River one night. Next to me sat an English-speaking Russian young fella, Alex, who I'd been talking with. I noticed that as the speaker was talking, this young man was really giving me the visual once-over. Then he asked pointedly, "Norman, are you an American big shot?"

I swallowed a laugh and said, "Maybe to a few people I am, but not in God's way of looking at us." I explained to Alex that God is not partial to one person over another. I began to think about that and how wonderful that truth is. As the Scriptures say, "But as many as received Him, to them He gave the right to become children of God" (John 1:12).

God offers Himself to *everyone*, and He has mandated us to share that miraculous truth with everyone we possibly can.

So, the bottom line of all this for me is that in these years God has given me, the maximum fulfillment is to love and honor God . . . through actually seeking to love others. That begins with sharing the truth of Christ with them and trying to help them hook up with Him!

If you've read this far, then you certainly have seen how God has made this a life beyond the "norm" for me. How about you?

APPENDIX ONE:
THE MISSION STATEMENT OF INTERSTATE
BATTERIES SYSTEM OF AMERICA

Mission

Our mission is to supply our customers worldwide with top quality, value-priced batteries and related electrical-power-source products and to provide our distributors and IBSA (Interstate Batteries System of America) with businesses which are profitable, rewarding, and growth oriented.

Philosophy

Our business philosophy is to treat others as we want to be treated, to treat all our business associates with respect, with fairness, with integrity, caring for and listening to them, professionally serving them, always being a model of working hard and striving toward excellence.

Our *customers* (distributors, dealers, and consumers) are our first priority. Therefore, we are committed to:

- treat them the way we want to be treated—honestly and with sincerity in every situation
- listen to them
- provide distributors with a rewarding business opportunity and aggressively serve them to enhance their success
- provide dealers with a profitable, comprehensive replacement battery program that best serves the customer

We care about our *employees*—physically, emotionally, financially, and spiritually. We are committed to:

- treat employees the way we want to be treated by acting with respect, integrity, and sincerity in every situation

- listen to our employees
- provide rewarding jobs and give each employee the opportunity to reach his or her personal and professional goals within a framework of fair compensation
- communicate goals and expectations clearly, hold employees accountable for achieving their goals, and reward them appropriately
- set an excellent example of commitment to company goals through hard work, honesty, loyalty, professionalism, and respect in all of management's dealings with them
- create an enjoyable working environment that is fulfilling and challenges them toward excellence
- provide competent management whose actions are just, ethical, and in adherence to biblical principles
- provide opportunities for study, growth, and outreach within a reasonable business framework

We acknowledge a responsibility to the *communities* in which we live and work. Therefore, we are committed to:

- serve as an example to our community and beyond by delivering excellence with integrity and humility
- be good citizens who exercise exemplary stewardship in support of good works and godly concerns
- support and promote responsible government
- bear our fair share of taxes

We are committed to enhancing our *stockholders'* investment. Therefore, we will:

- maintain a high level of accountability to our stockholders
- operate within a growth framework that ensures a fair return on their investment
- act as good stewards in handling the assets of the corporation

APPENDIX TWO:
MINISTRIES THAT DESERVE SUPPORT

In chapters 13 through 17 I share with you our giving philosophy and provide some accounts of how we have implemented our beliefs in this regard. I have invited a number of ministries to participate in this appendix material to answer any questions that might arise in the minds of readers as to the nature and extent of their work, and to provide addresses and pertinent information for those who might wish to contact these ministries themselves.

The *Jesus* Film Project

The *Jesus* Film Project of Campus Crusade for Christ International serves as the catalyst for the international distribution of the evangelistic film *Jesus.* The two-hour dramatic film accurately and creatively presents the life and message of Christ, as recorded in Luke's Gospel. In more than two hundred countries, both missionaries and nationals use the 320 language versions currently available, with 150 more in production. Viewers have surpassed 750 million. Where responses can be recorded, 10 to 30 percent of those watching the film have indicated a desire to know Christ personally, depending on the area of the world.

In North America many churches are now banding together to offer a free copy of the *Jesus* video to every home in their community.

Directed by Paul Eshleman, the *Jesus* Film Project staff believe that everyone deserves at least one chance to hear the good news of God's love and forgiveness in Christ. To that end, and in cooperation with churches and other Christian organizations, its goals include completing 1,154 language versions of *Jesus.* Local and international donor gifts undergird the strategic use of *Jesus* by national film teams to reach their own nations for the Savior. For more information, please contact:

The *Jesus* Film Project
P.O. Box 72007
San Clemente, CA 92674
Phone: (714)361-7575
FAX: (714)361-7579

Dallas Theological Seminary

Founded in 1924, Dallas Theological Seminary is committed to studying, understanding, and applying the truth of the Bible to everyday life. As the fourth president of the seminary, Dr. Charles R. Swindoll continues the school's mission as a professional, graduate-level school, preparing men and women for service as godly servants/leaders in the Body of Christ worldwide.

A fully accredited institution offering ten master's and doctoral degree programs, Dallas Theological Seminary has graduated more than eight thousand students from all fifty states and over eighty countries. Because it is not affiliated with any one denomination, it is dependent on the prayers and financial support of all those who share its beliefs and goal of producing graduates who can handle God's Word accurately and practically. For information, write or call:

Dallas Theological Seminary
3909 Swiss Avenue
Dallas, TX 75204
Phone: (214)824-3094

Overseas Council International

Overseas Council for Theological Education and Missions, Inc., was organized in 1974 by business and professional people as well as mission and church leaders, who believe that the nations of the world can best be reached by their own sons and daughters. Convinced that the seminary is the heart of the church and charts the future theological emphasis of multiple denominations, Overseas Council assists fifty-four strategically positioned evangelical training institutions in the developing countries of the world. It is this part of our world where the need for trained laborers is so great, because of an unprecedented harvest. These centers represent a student body in excess of fourteen thousand from ninety-six countries and 590 denominations and organizations.

Overseas Council International consists of affiliates in Canada, the British Isles, Europe, South Africa, Australia, New Zealand, and the United States.

Financial support by Overseas Council is given in the forms of scholarships, capital funds, libraries, faculty support, and advanced education for professors. Training of future leaders of the church is considered one of the best bargains in missions today. For more information, contact:

Dr. Charles Spicer
Overseas Council International
P.O. Box 751
Greenwood, IN 46142
Phone: (317)882-4174
FAX: (317)882-4195

Global Missions Fellowship (GMF)

"To see the Great Commission fulfilled in our lifetime" is the battle cry and visionary ministry thrust of Global Missions Fellowship. What began as obedience to Christ's Great Commission in the heart of Mike Downey, president and founder of GMF, has blossomed into a worldwide harvest of churches.

GMF is characterized as a "through the church" ministry that exists to serve the church around the world as a catalyst to plant new churches in major urban areas. By mobilizing teams of pastors and laypersons to serve on a seven- to ten-day basis, GMF conducts evangelistic campaigns that help establish new congregations. Since its beginning in 1984, GMF lay teams have planted over nine hundred churches in forty-five countries on five continents and have seen more than 70,000 professions of faith in Jesus Christ.

We believe that the Great Commission will be literally fulfilled in our lifetime by mobilizing the church to focus her resources on evangelism that results in planting new churches. Just as the apostle Paul established new churches by proclaiming the gospel in the cities of his day, GMF is a servant to the Body of Christ to help her maximize her mission mandate.

For further information, please contact:

Mike Downey, founder and president
Global Missions Fellowship
P.O. Box 742828
Dallas, TX 75374
Phone: (214)783-7476
FAX: (214)234-4960

Bill Glass Prison Ministry

To launch an effective prison ministry, Bill Glass knew he must plan and organize a strategy that would command the attention of the most hardened criminal. He scheduled top speakers, musicians, and athletes such as Roger Staubach, Coach Tom Landry of the Dallas Cowboys, and Mike Singletary of the Chicago Bears for special in-prison shows and presentations called "Weekend of Champions." The idea is to have prominent individuals and sports figures to help attract the attention of as many inmates as possible.

Each program is followed by intense, one-on-one witnessing by a team of volunteer lay counselors who have completed several hours of training for this important task. The plan has proven to be highly successful. Today, the "Weekend of Champions" programs are conducted in as many as ten prisons most weekends with 150 to 1,100 volunteer counselors participating. Each year the team visits over 175 different prisons.

The lifeblood of our ministry is the counselors who come from across the U.S., taking time out of their busy lives and paying their own way to share Christ with the inmates for two and a half days. In the cells, over meals, and out in the yard, they deal with the broken lives, empty hearts, and shattered dreams of men and women—the result of a society that has turned its back on God.

For more information, contact:

Bill Glass Prison Ministry
P.O. Box 9000
Cedar Hill, TX 75104-9000
Phone: (214)291-7895
FAX: (214)293-0173

World Impact

World Impact is a Christian missions organization dedicated to ministering God's love to the inner cities of America. Its purpose is to honor and glorify God and delight in Him in the inner cities by knowing God and making Him known through evangelism, follow-up, discipleship, and planting culturally-conducive churches.

World Impact ministers cross-culturally in the inner city to people unreached by the gospel of Jesus Christ and trains indigenous Christian leadership for the advancement of the kingdom of God.

For more information, contact:

Dr. Keith Phillips, founder and president
World Impact, Inc.
2001 South Vermont Avenue
Los Angeles, CA 90007
Phone: (213)735-1137

Doulos Ministries, Inc.

Doulos Ministries is a one-year, life-changing discipleship training program for college-graduate-age young men and women. The Doulos participants receive weekly classroom teaching, hands-on ministry training with youth and families, and an opportunity to serve in the community. The organization chose the Greek word *doulos* as its name because it pictures a slave who has obtained freedom, yet willingly continues to serve his master out of love for him. Following the apostle Paul, Doulos Ministries act as the bond servants of Jesus Christ in response to His tremendous love.

One of the ministries used in its training is Shelterwood, a residential care center for adolescents in crisis, operated by Doulos Ministries. Doulos and Shelterwood are located in Branson, Missouri, and in Denver, Colorado. For more information, please contact:

Richard A. Beach
Doulos Ministries, Inc.
5500 East Yale Ave., Fourth Floor
Denver, CO 80222
Phone: (303)254-9278

Prison Fellowship Ministries

Founded in 1976 by former Nixon aide and Watergate figure Charles Colson, Prison Fellowship (PF) is a nonprofit, volunteer-reliant organization focused on one overriding vision: that all those involved in and directly impacted by crime will experience the grace and peace of Jesus Christ. Its mission is to exhort, assist, and equip the church in its ministry to prisoners, ex-prisoners, victims, and their families, and in its advancement of biblical standards of justice. To that end, PF recruits, trains, and mobilizes volunteers from a variety of denominations and backgrounds to participate in a wide range of in-prison and community programs. To date, more than fifty thousand trained volunteers are active in prison and community programs, such as family and spouse support groups and ex-prisoner mentoring matches.

In particular, PF attempts to help offenders turn their lives around through evangelism, discipleship, and practical assistance. As founder and chairman of the board, Chuck Colson is actively involved in the work, visiting prisons regularly and working with the top-level leadership to help guide PF's mission and priorities.

PF is an international ministry with more than sixty countries hosting active, chartered PF ministries, making it the world's largest movement working in and out of prisons in a multifaceted strategy to break the cycle of crime. All PF programs are designed to effect restoration—bringing healing and the peace of Christ to individuals, families, and communities.

For more information, please contact:

Prison Fellowship Ministries
P.O. Box 17500
Washington, D.C. 20041-0500
Phone: (703)478-0100
FAX: (703)478-0452

Luis Palau Evangelistic Association

The Luis Palau Evangelistic Association (LPEA) is a Christian ministry of evangelism. In dependence upon God, LPEA wants to win as many people as possible to Jesus Christ throughout the world, proclaiming His good news by all available means to the millions of people who have yet to respond to the gospel.

Now well into his third decade of mass evangelism, evangelist Luis Palau has spoken to hundreds of millions of people in ninety-five nations through radio and television broadcasts, and in person to eleven million in sixty-three nations.

For more information, please contact:

Mike Umlandt,
senior editor and public relations coordinator
Luis Palau Evangelistic Association
P.O. Box 1173
Portland, OR 97207-1173
Phone: (503)614-1500
FAX: (503)614-1599

Search Ministries

For nearly two decades Search Ministries has been involved in lovingly communicating the claims of Christ to both believers and seekers. The mission was founded with the conviction that adults could be reached with the message of God's love in a natural and informal way through open forums, small groups, retreats, and one-on-one situations. These creative vehicles provide an open, affirming atmosphere that allows people to clarify and understand the claims of Christ and make life-changing decisions.

Search seeks to help adults develop spiritually and have an impact in their sphere of influence. Through seminars, conferences, small groups, and individual training, people are equipped to grow in their relationship with God and to skillfully express that relationship in their homes, neighborhoods, places of employment, and leisure pursuits.

A variety of publications and training materials are available to facilitate the equipping of believers in the areas of Christian apologetics, lifestyle evangelism, and basic discipleship. Materials are also available for use with seekers, such as investigative Bible studies and apologetic booklets.

Search Ministries currently has area directors in many major cities across the United States. Together, their common purpose is to assist in fulfilling the Great Commission by involving adults in the process of lifestyle evangelism and discipleship through modeling and training. For more information, please write or call:

Search Ministries
5038 Dorsey Hall Drive
Ellicott City, MD 21042
Phone: (410)740-5300

CoMission

The objective of CoMission is to mobilize a Christian peace corps consisting of educators and laypeople to introduce the people of the former Soviet Union to the life-changing power of God's Word.

CoMission's strategy is to place these individuals in teams of ten throughout the 150 school districts of the former Soviet Union to live for one year during a five-year period. Their goals are to expose teachers to a course in Christian morality and ethics, start community Bible classes, and develop relationships with national leadership. The anticipated result will be a significant rebuilding of schools, families, and society on the truths of God's Word.

The end goal is to pass the "baton" on to trained national Christians (Russians, Ukrainians, Latvians, Romanians, Estonians, etc.) who will ensure their republics move forward on the truths of Scripture for generations to come. For further information, please contact:

King A. Crow
CoMission Headquarters
760 Heritage Parkway
Fort Mill, SC 29715
Phone: (803)547-3838
FAX: (803)547-3835

BEE World (Biblical Education by Extension)

In numerous countries, men and women who faithfully serve the Lord regularly face opposition and persecution for their faith in Jesus Christ. These servants of Christ call out for help from the church in

---

the West. They especially request help in practical Biblical training for their present and future leaders.

BEE came into existence to respond to this need. It is an intermission, interdenominational ministry committed to assisting the national church in the establishment of church-based training centers that will provide training for now and the future. BEE serves the church in China, Vietnam, and other restricted-access countries.

For more information, write to:

BEE World
228 N. Cascade, Suite 308
Colorado Springs, CO 80903
E-mail: CompuServe, 72217,2031

APPENDIX THREE:
THE FOUR SPIRITUAL LAWS[1]

Just as there are physical laws that govern the physical universe, so are there spiritual laws that govern your relationship with God.

(References contained in this section should be read in context from the Bible wherever possible.)

1
LAW ONE
*God **loves** you and offers a wonderful **plan** for your life.*

God's Love
"For God so loved the world, that He gave His only begotten Son, that whoever believes in Him should not perish, but have eternal life" (John 3:16).

God's Plan
[Christ speaking:] "I came that they might have life, and might have it abundantly" [that it might be full and meaningful] (John 10:10).

Why is it that most people are not experiencing the abundant life? Because . . .

2
LAW TWO
*Man is **sinful** and **separated** from God. Thus he cannot know and experience God's love and plan for his life.*

Man Is Sinful

"For all have sinned and fall short of the glory of God" (Romans 3:23).

Man was created to have fellowship with God; but, because of his stubborn self-will, he chose to go his own independent way, and fellowship with God was broken. This self-will, characterized by an attitude of active rebellion or passive indifference, is an evidence of what the Bible calls sin.

Man Is Separated

"For the wages of sin is death" [spiritual separation from God] (Romans 6:23).

This diagram illustrates that God is holy and man is sinful. A great gulf separates the two. The arrows illustrate that man is continually trying to reach God and the abundant life through his own efforts, such as a good life, philosophy, or religion.

The Third Law explains the only way to bridge this gulf . . .

Law Three

*Jesus Christ is God's **only** provision for man's sin. Through Him you can know and experience God's love and plan for your life.*

He Died in Our Place

"But God demonstrates His own love toward us, in that while we were yet sinners, Christ died for us" (Romans 5:8).

He Rose from the Dead

"Christ died for our sins. . . . He was buried. . . . He was raised on the third day, according to the Scriptures. . . . He appeared to Peter, then to the twelve. After that He appeared to more than five hundred" (1 Corinthians 15:3-6).

He Is the Only Way to God

"Jesus said to him, 'I am the way, and the truth, and the life; no one comes to the Father, but through Me'" (John 14:6).

This diagram illustrates that God has bridged the gulf that separates us from Him by sending His Son, Jesus Christ, to die on the cross in our place to pay the penalty for our sins.

It is not enough just to know these three laws . . .

Law Four

*We must individually **receive** Jesus Christ as Savior and Lord; then we can know and experience God's love and plan for our lives.*

We Must Receive Christ

"But as many as received Him, to them He gave the right to become children of God, even to those who believe in His name" (John 1:12).

We Receive Christ through Faith

"For by grace you have been saved through faith; and that not of yourselves, it is the gift of God; not as a result of works, that no one should boast" (Ephesians 2:8-9).

When We Receive Christ, We Experience a New Birth

(Read John 3:1-8.)

We Receive Christ by Personal Invitation

[Christ speaking:] "Behold, I stand at the door and knock; if any one hears My voice and opens the door, I will come in to him" (Revelation 3:20).

Receiving Christ involves turning to God from self (repentance) and trusting Christ to come into our lives to forgive our sins and to make us the kind of people He wants us to be. Just to agree intellectually that Jesus Christ is the Son of God and that He died on the cross for our sins is not enough. Nor is it enough to have an emotional experience. We receive Jesus Christ by faith, as an act of the will.

These two circles represent two kinds of lives:

Self-Directed Life
S—Self is on the throne
†—Christ is outside the life
•—Interests are directed by self,
  often resulting in discord and frustration

Christ-Directed Life
†—Christ is in the life and on the throne
S—Self is yielding to Christ
•—Interests are directed by Christ,
  resulting in harmony with God's plan

Which circle best represents your life? Which circle would you like to have represent your life?
The following explains how you can receive Christ . . .

You Can Receive Christ Right Now by Faith through Prayer

(*Prayer* is talking with God.)

God knows your heart and is not so concerned with your words as He is with the attitude of your heart. The following is a suggested prayer:

Lord Jesus, I need You. Thank You for dying on the cross for my sins. I open the door of my life and receive You as my Savior and Lord. Thank You for forgiving my sins and giving me eternal life. Take control of the throne of my life. Make me the kind of person You want me to be.

Does this prayer express the desire of your heart? If it does, pray this prayer right now, and Christ will come into your life, as He promised.

How to Know That Christ Is in Your Life

Did you receive Christ into your life? According to His promise in Revelation 3:20, where is Christ right now in relation to you? Christ said that He would come into your life. Would He mislead you? On what authority do you know that God has answered your prayer? (The trustworthiness of God Himself and His Word.)

The Bible Promises Eternal Life to All Who Receive Christ

And the witness is this, that God has given us eternal life, and this life is in His Son. He who has the Son has the life; he who does not have the Son of God does not have the life. These things I have written to you who believe in the name of the Son of God, in order that you may know that you have eternal life. (1 John 5:11-13)

Thank God often that Christ is in your life and that He will never leave you (Hebrews 13:5). You can know on the basis of His promise that Christ lives in you and that you have eternal life, from the very moment you invite Him in. He will not deceive you.

An important reminder . . .

Do Not Depend upon Feelings

The promise of God's Word, the Bible—not our feelings—is our authority. The Christian lives by faith (trust) in the trustworthiness of God Himself and His Word. This train diagram illustrates the relationship between *fact* (God and His Word), *faith* (our trust in God and His Word), and *feeling* (the result of our faith and obedience) (John 14:21).

The train will run with or without the caboose. However, it would be useless to attempt to pull the train by the caboose. In the same way, we, as Christians, do not depend on feelings or emotions, but we place our faith (trust) in the trustworthiness of God and the promises of His Word.

Now That You Have Received Christ

The moment that you received Christ by faith, as an act of the will, many things happened, including the following:

1. Christ came into your life (Revelation 3:20; Colossians 1:27).
2. Your sins were forgiven (Colossians 1:14).
3. You became a child of God (John 1:12).
4. You received eternal life (John 5:24).
5. You began the great adventure for which God created you (John 10:10; 2 Corinthians 5:17; 1 Thessalonians 5:18).

Can you think of anything more wonderful that could happen to you than receiving Christ? Would you like to thank God in prayer right now for what He has done for you? By thanking God, you demonstrate your faith.

To enjoy your new life to the fullest . . .

Suggestions for Christian Growth

Spiritual growth results from trusting Jesus Christ. "The righteous man shall live by faith" (Galatians 3:11). A life of faith will enable you to trust God increasingly with every detail of your life, and to practice the following:

G Go to God in prayer daily (John 15:7).

R Read God's Word daily (Acts 17:11)—begin with the Gospel of John.

O Obey God moment by moment (John 14:21).

W Witness for Christ by your life and words (Matthew 4:19; John 15:8).

T Trust God for every detail of your life (1 Peter 5:7).

H Holy Spirit—allow Him to control and empower your daily life and witness (Galatians 5:16-17; Acts 1:8).

Fellowship in a Good Church

God's Word admonishes us not to forsake "the assembling of ourselves together" (Hebrews 10:25). Several logs burn brightly together, but put one aside on the cold hearth, and the fire goes out. So it is with your relationship with other Christians. If you do not belong to a church, do not wait to be invited. Take the initiative; call the pastor of a nearby church where Christ is honored and His Word is preached. Start this week, and make plans to attend regularly.

Special Materials Are Available for Christian Growth

If you have come to know Christ personally through this presentation of the gospel, write for a free booklet written especially to assist you in your Christian growth.

A special Bible study series and an abundance of other helpful materials for Christian growth are also available. For additional information, please write: Campus Crusade for Christ International, San Bernardino, California 92414.

You will want to share this important discovery . . .

NOTES

Chapter 3

1. Myron Rush, *Lord of the Marketplace* (Wheaton, IL: Victor Books, 1986).

Chapter 7

1. Charles Swindoll, *The Quest for Character* (Grand Rapids, MI: Zondervan, 1993).

Chapter 9

1. Source unknown.

Chapter 15

1. William D. Lawrence with Jack A. Turpin, *Beyond the Bottom Line* (Chicago: Moody Press, Praxis Books, 1994), 109.

Chapter 17

1. Oswald Chambers, *My Utmost for His Highest* (New York: Dodd, Mead & Co., 1963), 304.
2. Charles Swindoll, *Simple Faith* (Dallas: Word Publishing, 1991), 53.
3. Swindoll, *Simple Faith,* 53.

Appendix Three

1. Written by Bill Bright. Copyright © 1965 Campus Crusade for Christ, Inc. All rights reserved. The *Four Spiritual Laws* booklet has been reprinted in its entirety. Therefore Scripture references have not been changed to reflect *The New American Standard* version of the Bible.

ABOUT THE AUTHOR

Norm Miller is the chairman of the board of Interstate Batteries, the number one replacement battery in America. Since beginning his career as a route salesman in 1962, He has moved through the ranks from his father's Tennessee distributorship to the helm of Interstate's executive management team. The experiences he has had, both business-wise and personal, have developed in him a deep faith and the guiding principles necessary for a truly successful life. He serves on the boards of Dallas Theological Seminary, Dallas Seminary Foundation, and Overseas Council USA and International.

He and his dear wife, Anne, Live in Dallas, Texas. They have two children and four grandchildren.